BOOKKEEPING MASTERY FOR SMALL BUSINESSES

7 QUICK & EASY ACCOUNTING STRATEGIES TO
MAXIMIZE PROFIT, MANAGE CASH FLOW, AND
SIMPLIFY TAX COMPLIANCE

D.K. BURNETT

CONTENTS

INTRODUCTION

In my three decades of navigating the intricate business management and accounting world, I've witnessed firsthand the dramatic impact effective bookkeeping can have on a business's fate. One case that stands out involved a small construction company teetering on the brink of failure. By implementing a few key bookkeeping strategies, not only did we steer it back to stability, but we also set it on a path to remarkable growth. This transformation was not just about numbers; it was about the people behind those numbers finally understanding and taking control of their financial destiny.

This book is born from a profound desire to make bookkeeping and financial management accessible and understandable for you, the small business owner. Far too often, the accounting world is shrouded in jargon and complexity, leaving many feeling overwhelmed and disconnected from their business's financial health. Here, we aim to change that narrative. This book demystifies managing your business finances effectively by combining practical strategies with real-world examples and explaining them in terms you can relate to.

My journey over the years, working across non-profit, construction, real estate, restaurant, daycare, and consulting industries, coupled with a solid academic foundation in accounting, has equipped me with a broad spectrum of experiences. It is these experiences, along with a passion for empowering small businesses, that I bring to you through these pages.

If the thought of bookkeeping fills you with dread, you're not alone. Many small business owners feel the same way. However, I'm here to reassure you that by the end of this book, you will have a solid grasp of bookkeeping fundamentals and feel empowered to make informed financial decisions for your business.

This book is your comprehensive roadmap to financial mastery, structured to guide you from bookkeeping basics to more advanced financial strategies for business growth. Along the way, you'll find practical tools such as templates, checklists, and software recommendations to streamline your bookkeeping processes.

By the time you turn the final page, you'll not only understand the importance of effective bookkeeping but also feel confident in your ability to implement these strategies for the success of your business.

I encourage you to approach this book with an open mind and a readiness to apply its lessons. The transformation in your financial management skills will, in turn, transform your business's success. Remember, mastering your finances is within your reach, and I am here to guide you every step of the way.

Let this be your moment of transformation. Let's demystify bookkeeping together and set your business on a path to achieving its goals. Here's to your success and the thrilling journey we'll embark on together.

1

DECODING FINANCIAL JARGON
FOR SMALL BUSINESS OWNERS

I n the bustling marketplace of ideas and innovation that characterizes the small business ecosystem, financial fluency is more than a mere advantage—it's the bedrock of building a sustainable enterprise. Amid the myriad responsibilities that fall on a small business owner's shoulders, understanding the financial basis of one's operation can seem daunting. However, this chapter aims to transform what might appear as a Herculean task into a series of manageable, understandable steps, enabling you to confidently navigate the financial landscape.

A common misconception among many is that bookkeeping and accounting are domains reserved for the number-savvy, those with an innate affinity for mathematics. This chapter challenges that notion head-on, breaking down fundamental financial terms and concepts into bite-sized, easily digestible pieces. Through this approach, the goal is not merely to acquaint you with these terms but to provide you with the tools to wield them effectively in the service of your business's financial health.

1.1 FROM LEDGERS TO LIQUIDITY: SIMPLIFYING ACCOUNTING TERMS

Understanding "Ledgers"

The term "ledger" might evoke images of dusty, leather-bound books, pages filled with obscure columns of numbers. In reality, a ledger serves a far more dynamic role in the life of your business. It is the central repository for recording all financial transactions your business undertakes. Each sale made, every expense incurred, and every payment received finds its way into the ledger, making it the heartbeat of your business's financial processes.

Consider the ledger as a detailed diary of your business's financial interactions with the world. Just as a diary offers a chronological account of events, providing insights into patterns and anomalies, a well-maintained ledger reveals the economic path of your business. It enables you to track growth, identify trends, and address potential issues before they escalate.

Demystifying "Liquidity"

"Liquidity" might sound like industry jargon reserved for the corridors of banks and investment firms. Yet, it denotes a concept as straightforward as it is crucial for the day-to-day operations of your business. Liquidity refers to your business's ability to quickly convert assets into cash, thereby meeting immediate and short-term financial obligations.

Imagine a scenario where your business needs to settle a sudden, unexpected expense—a scenario not uncommon in the unpredictable world of small business. Your ability to do so without disrupting your operations hinges on your business's liquidity.

High liquidity means having the flexibility to navigate unforeseen financial hurdles with ease, ensuring that your business remains on stable footing.

Clarifying "Assets vs. Liabilities"

Distinguishing between assets and liabilities is at the heart of financial management. Assets are what your business owns—be it cash, inventory, equipment, or property. They represent resources that hold value and are utilized to generate income. Liabilities are what your business owes to others, such as loans, mortgages, or unpaid bills. These are obligations that your business needs to settle in the future.

The interplay between assets and liabilities directly influences your business's net worth or equity. A robust understanding of this dynamic is pivotal. It allows you to make informed decisions regarding investments, borrowing, and expenditure, ensuring that your business's financial foundation remains solid.

Simplifying "Equity"

In a small business context, equity signifies the owner's financial stake in the enterprise. It is calculated by subtracting total liabilities from total assets. If this equation yields a positive number, your business has positive equity, indicating financial health and stability—conversely, negative equity—a scenario where liabilities exceed assets—signals potential financial distress.

Equity is not merely a figure on a balance sheet. It encapsulates the financial value of your sweat equity—every ounce of effort, every late night, and every strategic decision made to grow your business. It represents your claim on the business's assets after all liabilities have been satisfied. Understanding equity's significance is crucial for assessing your business's financial health and making strategic decisions that affect its growth and sustainability.

In navigating the financial landscape of your small business, these foundational concepts—ledgers, liquidity, assets, liabilities, and equity—serve as your compass. They equip you with the knowledge to make informed decisions, ensuring your business survives and thrives in the competitive marketplace. With this understanding, you can chart a course toward financial stability and growth, turning potential challenges into opportunities for success.

1.2 THE ABCS OF FINANCIAL STATEMENTS: BALANCE SHEETS, INCOME STATEMENTS, AND CASH FLOWS

Breaking Down "Balance Sheets"

Imagine your business as a complex machine. To understand how well it functions, you need a clear picture of its parts at any moment. This is where the balance sheet comes into play, offering a snapshot of your business's financial health by detailing its assets, liabilities, and equity. It's like taking a photograph; what you see is your business's financial position frozen at a specific point in time.

- Assets: This section lists everything of value your business owns. Think of it as the fuel that powers your business machine. Assets are typically categorized as current (cash or items that convert into cash within a year) or fixed (long-term assets, like equipment or real estate).
- Liabilities: Here, you'll find everything your business owes and the obligations it must meet. Like a gauge showing the pressure your business operates under, liabilities are

divided into current (due within a year) and long-term categories.

- Equity: This section reveals the owner's stake in the business after all liabilities have been paid off. It's the residual interest in the assets of the company.

JONES CONSULTING GROUP

Sample Balance Sheet

AS OF DECEMBER 15, 2013

Assets

Current Assets	
Checking Account	5,000
Savings Account	1,000
Petty Cash	500
Accounts Receivable	22,000
Inventory	15,000
Prepaid Insurance	6,000
Total Current Assets:	49,500
Non-Current Assets	
Accumulated Depreciation	-4,500
Computer, Office Equipment	7,000
Building	65,000
Land	60,000
Total Non-Current Assets:	127,500
Total Assets	177,000

Liabilities & Equity

Liabilities	
Current Liabilities	
Accounts Payable	12,000
Line of Credit	20,000
Payroll Liabilites	7,000
Total Current Liabilities:	39,000
Non-Current Liabilities	
Long-term Debt (loan)	48,000
Total Liabilities:	87,000
Equity	
Owner's Capital	35,000
Retained Earnings	55,000
Total Equity:	90,000
Total Liabilities & Equity	177,000

Understanding the balance sheet's components allows you to gauge your business's solvency and liquidity, offering insights into its ability to meet short and long-term obligations.

Understanding "Income Statements"

Transitioning from the static view provided by the balance sheet, the income statement, or profit and loss statement, plays out like a movie, depicting your business's financial performance over a period. It tells a story of how your business earns and spends money, encompassing its operational activities.

- Revenue: This top-line entry shows the total income generated from sales before deducting any expenses. The starting point is the gross income your business activities have produced.
- Expenses: Here, you'll account for the cost of goods sold (COGS) and operating expenses (rent, salaries, utilities), essentially, what it costs to run your business.
- Net Income: The climax of our story, net income, is calculated by subtracting expenses from revenue. It's what remains, indicating whether your business turned a profit or suffered a loss during the reporting period.

Income Statement

ACME Corporation
For the month ending 28 February 2014

	Current Period	YTD
Operating Income		
Product sales	29,540.32	57,243.00
Labor sales	4,232.04	8,108.57
Net Sales	33,772.36	65,351.57
Cost of Goods Sold	14,500.00	28,232.38
Gross Income	19,272.36	37,119.19
Operating Expenses		
Salaries	6,743.96	13,218.82
Advertising	432.32	1,404.21
Travel	100.08	243.00
Office	394.39	772.14
Other	92.99	99.94
Total Operating Expenses	7,763.74	15,738.11
Operating Income	11,508.62	21,381.08
Other Income & Expenses		
Other Income	118.13	224.23
Other Expenses	748.21	1,242.49
Total Other Income & Expenses	866.34	1,466.72
Net Income Before Taxes	10,642.28	19,914.36
Taxes	3,129.23	5,813.58
Net Income	7,513.05	14,100.78

This statement is crucial for understanding how your business's revenue streams and expense management strategies impact its bottom line.

Exploring "Cash Flow Statements"

While the income statement tells the story of your business's profitability, the cash flow statement reveals the tale of its liquidity, providing insights into the actual movement of cash in and out of your business. It's an essential tool for assessing the health of your business's heart – its cash flow.

- Operating Activities: This section records cash generated or spent in your business's core activities. It adjusts net income for non-cash items (such as depreciation, unrealized gains, or deferred expenses) and changes in working capital, giving a clear view of cash flow from day-to-day operations.
- Investing Activities: Here, you'll see cash used for or generated from buying or selling assets. This section offers insights into how your business is investing in its future growth and operational capacity.
- Financing Activities: This part details cash flow from borrowing, repaying debt, or equity financing activities. It reflects how your business raises capital and returns value to owners.

Cash Flow Statement
Diana's Goat Grooming
Month Ended January 31, 2019

Cash Flow from Operations

Net income	$60,000
Additions to Cash	
Depreciation	$20,000
Increase in Accounts Payable	$10,000
Subtractions from Cash	
Increase in Accounts Receivable	($20,000)
Increase in inventory	($30,000)
Net Cash from Operations	$40,000
Cash Flow from Investing	
Purchase of equipment	($5,000)
Cash Flow from Financing	
Notes payable	$7,500
Cash Flow for Month Ended December 31, 2018	$42,500

Effectively managing your cash flow statement can help ensure your business has the liquidity to cover its obligations and invest in growth opportunities.

Interpreting Financial Statements Together

When viewed in isolation, each financial statement provides valuable insights into different aspects of your business's economic health. However, when interpreting these documents together, a comprehensive picture emerges.

- Balance Sheet and Income Statement: The balance sheet gives you a snapshot of your business at a point in time, while the income statement shows how your business performed over time. By comparing these statements, you can observe how your business's performance impacts its financial position.
- Income Statement and Cash Flow Statement: While the income statement shows profitability, the cash flow statement reveals if your profitable operations generate sufficient cash to sustain and grow your business. This comparison helps identify whether income is tied up in non-cash elements or expenses that consume your cash.
- Balance Sheet and Cash Flow Statement: Comparing these can help you understand how your assets, liabilities, and equity changes affect your cash flow. For instance, an increase in liabilities might indicate new debt taken on, reflected as a cash inflow in the financing section of your cash flow statement.

Combining the information from these three statements gives you a multidimensional view of your business's financial health, encompassing its profitability, solvency, and liquidity. This holistic understanding is indispensable for making informed decisions that steer your company toward sustainable growth and stability.

1.3 COMMON BOOKKEEPING TERMS EVERY SMALL BUSINESS OWNER SHOULD KNOW

Grasping "Debits and Credits"

In the mechanics of bookkeeping, debits and credits are the fundamental operations that keep the financial engine of your business humming. Simply put, every transaction your business engages in will either increase or decrease the value of different accounts, classified under assets, liabilities, or equity. Debits and credits are the tools that make these adjustments.

- Debits: Imagine debits as the financial equivalent of inhaling, drawing resources into an account. When you debit an asset account, its value increases, allowing your business to accumulate resources. Conversely, debiting a liability or equity account reduces its value or decreases a financial burden.
- Credits: Credits, on the other hand, can be likened to exhaling, releasing resources from an account. Crediting an asset account decreases its value while crediting a liability or equity account increases its value, similar to enhancing your financial stability or capacity to invest.

The golden rule here is that for every transaction, the total amount debited must always equal the total amount credited, maintaining the balance central to double-entry bookkeeping. This system creates a comprehensive and self-balancing overview of all financial transactions, providing a clear picture of your business's financial health.

Understanding "Journal Entries"

Journal entries are the building blocks of your business's financial records, meticulously documenting the flow of transactions. Think of them as diary entries that capture the financial narrative of your business, recording the details of every transaction, including the date, accounts affected, and amounts of debits and credits.

Typically, creating a journal entry involves:

- Identifying transactions: Every financial activity is recorded, from paying rent to receiving payment from a customer.
- Analyzing transactions: Determine which accounts are affected and whether each should be debited or credited.
- Recording entries: Enter the transactions into the journal, ensuring that the debits equal the credits for each entry.

Journal Entry Examples

On December 1, 2023, Mr. Richard Anderson started Anderson Consulting Services by investing $15,000.

The journal entry increases the cash and increases (establishes) the capital account of Mr. Anderson.

Date 2023	Account	Debit	Credit
Dec 1	Cash	15,000.00	
	Mr. Anderson, Capital		15,000.00

On December 7, the company acquired tables, chairs, shelves, and other fixtures for $2,500. They paid for the purchase in cash.

Increase the asset account (Furniture and Fixtures) and decrease another asset account (Cash).

Date 2023	Account	Debit	Credit
Dec 7	Furniture and Fixtures	2,500.00	
	Cash		2,500.00

This process transforms raw financial data into a structured format, providing the foundation for all subsequent financial reporting and analysis. Through these journal entries, the intricate web of your business's financial activities is woven, laying bare the patterns of income and expenditure that drive your business forward.

Navigating "Accounts Receivable and Payable"

The terms "Accounts Receivable" and "Accounts Payable" are central to managing the lifeblood of your business: cash flow. They represent the yin and yang of your business transactions, capturing the balance between money flowing into and out of your business.

- Accounts Receivable: This account tracks money owed to your business for goods or services delivered but not yet paid for. The promise of future cash inflows is a critical asset that fuels your business operations. Efficient accounts receivable management involves timely billing, follow-ups on outstanding invoices, and strategies to minimize late payments, ensuring that your business maintains a steady cash flow.
- Accounts Payable: This account records the money your business owes to suppliers or creditors for goods or

services received but not yet paid. It signifies upcoming cash outflows, obligations your business must meet to sustain its operations and uphold its reputation. Prudent management of accounts payable entails organizing payments to avoid late fees while optimizing cash flow, negotiating payment terms, and taking advantage of any available discounts for early payment.

Together, these accounts act as the gatekeepers of your cash flow, and their management is pivotal to maintaining the financial equilibrium of your business.

Deciphering "Accruals"

Accruals stand at the crossroads of accounting and reality, recording revenues earned and expenses incurred regardless of whether cash has changed hands. This concept is a cornerstone of the accrual basis of accounting, which stipulates that financial events are recognized when they occur, not necessarily when cash is received or paid.

This approach to accounting offers several advantages:

- Revenue Recognition: Accruals allow for revenue recognition at the time earned, providing a more accurate picture of financial performance. For example, if you complete a project in December but don't receive payment until January, the revenue is recognized in December, aligning income with the effort expended.
- Expense Matching: Similarly, recording expenses when incurred ensures they match the revenue they help generate. This might mean recognizing the cost of materials when used in production, not when paid for,

offering a true reflection of costs associated with revenue.

Accruals play a critical role in financial reporting, ensuring that financial statements reflect the economic reality of your business activities and providing insights into its operational efficiency and profitability. They bridge the gap between the financial transactions that drive your business and the underlying events, ensuring your financial statements are a true compass guiding your business decisions.

1.4 DECIPHERING TAX JARGON: WHAT YOU NEED TO KNOW

Tax season can evoke anticipation and anxiety for small business owners. With its unique language, the maze of tax laws and regulations often seems designed to confuse rather than clarify. However, understanding a few key concepts can significantly demystify this process, turning a source of stress into an opportunity to optimize your business's financial health.

Understanding "Tax Deductions"

Tax deductions serve as a buffer between your business's gross income and your taxable amount. They consist of business expenses that the IRS allows you to subtract from your total income. Deductions lower your taxable income, which, in turn, can significantly reduce your tax bill. It's like receiving a discount on your taxes for certain business expenditures.

For instance, if your business earns $100,000 during the year and you have $30,000 in deductible expenses, you'll only be taxed on $70,000. Deductions can range from rent, utilities, and office supplies to more complex expenditures like depreciation. The key is to maintain meticulous records of these expenses, as they play a pivotal role in your tax strategy, potentially saving you a considerable amount in taxes.

Navigating "Tax Credits"

While tax deductions lower the amount of taxable income, tax credits directly reduce your tax bill, dollar-for-dollar. Think of them as a gift card from the IRS: if you're eligible for a $1,000 tax credit and owe $3,000 in taxes, you'll only pay $2,000. Tax credits encourage specific business activities beneficial to the economy or environment, such as hiring veterans, investing in research and development, or utilizing renewable energy sources.

The impact of tax credits on your tax liability can be substantial. However, navigating which credits you're eligible for and how to claim them requires a solid understanding of their rules. It's often worth consulting with a tax professional to ensure you're leveraging every available credit, as this can significantly lower your overall tax burden.

Demystifying "Quarterly Taxes"

For many small business owners, the concept of quarterly taxes represents a shift from the once-a-year tax filing customary to individuals. The IRS requires businesses and self-employed individuals to pay estimated quarterly taxes if they expect to owe at least $1,000 in taxes for the year. This system is comparable to a "pay-as-you-go" model, designed to spread tax payments throughout the year, making them more manageable and avoiding a large lump sum come April.

Paying quarterly taxes involves estimating your income, deductions, and credits for the year and dividing the anticipated tax due into four payments. While calculating your tax liability may seem daunting, it prevents cash flow surprises and penalties for underpayment. Tools and resources are available, including IRS worksheets (Form 1040-ES, found on the IRS website) and software to help calculate these estimated payments. Staying proactive with quarterly taxes ensures that you're not caught off guard, allowing for smoother financial planning throughout the year.

Grasping "Employment Taxes"

When you have employees, your tax responsibilities include withholding and paying employment taxes. These taxes include federal income tax, Social Security and Medicare taxes (collectively known as FICA taxes), and federal unemployment tax (FUTA). Essentially, you're acting as an intermediary, collecting taxes from your employees' wages and paying them to the government.

- Federal Income Tax: Withhold based on each employee's W-4 form and the IRS withholding tables.
- Social Security and Medicare Taxes: Both you and your employees contribute, with each party paying half of the total due. The combined rate for Social Security and Medicare taxes is 15.3%, split evenly between employer and employee.
- Federal Unemployment Tax (FUTA): Unlike the other employment taxes, FUTA is paid only by employers and is used to fund state workforce agencies.

Navigating employment taxes involves meticulous payroll management and understanding current tax rates and regulations. Regularly reviewing these obligations helps ensure compliance, preventing costly penalties and contributing to the financial stability of your employees and business.

Tackling the tax responsibilities of a small business can initially seem like navigating through a maze. However, with a clear understanding of deductions, credits, quarterly taxes, and employment taxes, you transform these obligations into opportunities. Opportunities to optimize your tax strategy, maintain compliance, and ultimately support your business's financial health and growth. By clarifying these aspects of taxation, you're better equipped to navigate the complexities of the tax landscape, ensuring that your business survives and thrives in the competitive marketplace.

1.5 MAKING SENSE OF PAYROLL: A GLOSSARY FOR THE NON-ACCOUNTANT

Payroll is more than just cutting checks or setting up direct deposits for your employees. It's a critical function that touches on accounting, human resources, and legal compliance. Small business owners, especially those without a background in finance or accounting, might find payroll to be a complex landscape to navigate. This section aims to explain payroll simply, breaking it down into its fundamental components.

Breaking Down "Gross vs. Net Pay"

Two terms frequently come up when processing payroll: gross pay and net pay. The distinction between these pay types is crucial for you and your employees to understand.

- Gross Pay: This represents an employee's total earnings before any deductions are made. It includes all forms of compensation, such as salaries, wages, bonuses, and overtime pay.
- Net Pay: Often referred to as "take-home pay," net pay is what remains after all deductions, taxes, and employee contributions to benefits are subtracted from gross pay. Net pay is the actual amount that appears on an employee's paycheck or in their bank account through direct deposit.

Calculating Net Pay Example

To calculate the net pay for an hourly employee, you need to subtract any applicable payroll deductions from their gross pay.

Assuming the hourly rate for an employee is $20, they worked 40 hours plus 5 hours of overtime during the week.

First, calculate the employee's gross pay for the week by multiplying their hourly rate by the number of regular hours worked:

Earnings	**$950.00**
Hourly (40 hrs × $20.00)	$800.00
Overtime (1.5 × 5 hrs × $20.00)	$150.00
Taxes	**-$185.66**
Federal Income Tax	-$69.83
Social Security Tax	-$58.90
Medicare Tax	-$13.78
State Income Tax	-$38.87
Local Tax	-$4.28
Benefits	**-$66.50**
401(k)	-$66.50
Take Home	**$697.84**

Regular Pay = $20 per hour x 40 hours = $800
Overtime Pay = ($20 x 1.5 times) x 5 hours = $150
Gross Income = $950

Next, calculate the employee's payroll deductions for the week. This will vary based on several factors, such as their tax withholding status, benefit elections, and any other pre/post-tax deductions they have.

Assuming the total deductions for this employee amounts to $252.16.

Lastly, subtract the total deductions from the gross pay to arrive at the net pay:

$950 gross pay – $ 252.16 deductions = $697.84 net pay

It's important to note that these calculations may vary depending on the specific deductions and tax laws in your state/county/city.

Understanding the difference between gross and net pay is vital for explaining pay stubs to your employees and for accurate bookkeeping and tax reporting.

Understanding "Withholding Taxes"

One of the key responsibilities you take on when processing payroll is withholding taxes from your employee's wages. These taxes include federal income tax, state and local taxes (where applicable), and FICA taxes (Social Security and Medicare).

- The amount withheld for federal income tax is determined by the information your employees provide on their W-4 forms. Their filing status, number of dependents, and any additional withholding they request are considered.
- FICA taxes are more straightforward, with fixed Social Security and Medicare percentages split evenly between the employer and employee.

Ensuring accurate withholding is critical to avoid underpayment penalties for your employees and to keep your business compliant with tax regulations.

Navigating "Payroll Periods"

The frequency with which you pay your employees—your payroll period—can significantly affect your business operations. Standard payroll periods include weekly, bi-weekly, semi-monthly, and monthly. The choice of payroll period affects:

- Cash flow: More frequent payroll periods can strain cash flow, requiring you to have enough cash on hand more often.
- Employee satisfaction: Employees might have preferences based on their financial planning needs.
- Administrative workload: The frequency of payroll directly impacts the workload of your payroll administration, with more frequent periods requiring more processing time.

Selecting the correct payroll period is a balancing act between meeting legal requirements, managing cash flow, accommodating employee preferences, and minimizing administrative burdens.

Deciphering "Employee Benefits"

Beyond wages, employee benefits are a crucial part of the compensation package you offer your team. Benefits include health insurance, retirement plans, paid time off, and other non-wage compensations. While providing a robust benefits package can help attract and retain top talent, managing these benefits adds another layer of complexity to payroll processing.

- Health Insurance: If you offer health insurance, the employee might pay part of the premium through payroll deductions. Managing these deductions requires staying up-to-date with enrollment changes and premium adjustments.

- Retirement Plans: Contributions to retirement plans, such as a 401(k), are another common payroll deduction. You might also match employees' contributions to some extent, further complicating payroll calculations.
- Paid time Off (PTO): Tracking and managing PTO accrual and usage is another aspect of payroll. Ensuring that employees are correctly compensated for their time off requires meticulous record-keeping.

Properly managing benefits contributes to employee satisfaction and ensures compliance with various regulations that govern employee benefits, such as the Affordable Care Act for health insurance and ERISA for retirement plans.

In conclusion, mastering payroll is a multifaceted challenge that encompasses understanding key concepts such as gross vs. net pay, accurately withholding taxes, choosing appropriate payroll periods, and managing employee benefits. Each element is critical in ensuring your payroll process is seamless, compliant, and supportive of your business and employees' needs. Though the landscape may seem complex, breaking it into manageable components can help demystify payroll, making running your small business less daunting.

2

ESTABLISHING YOUR BOOKKEEPING SYSTEM

I magine you're standing at a crossroads; one path is well-trodden and straightforward but possibly limiting, and the other is less visible, requiring more effort to navigate but promising greater rewards in terms of insights and control over your financial landscape. This crossroads represents the choice between cash-basis and accrual-basis accounting methods. Each has its merits and drawbacks, and understanding these is crucial for plotting the financial course of your business.

2.1 CHOOSING THE RIGHT BOOKKEEPING METHOD FOR YOUR BUSINESS: CASH VS. ACCRUAL

Understanding "Cash Basis" Accounting

Cash basis accounting is similar to keeping track of your checkbook. Revenue is recognized when cash physically enters your account, and expenses are recorded when cash leaves. It's straightforward:

- Visibility: You have a clear picture of cash flow at any given moment. It's like checking your wallet; what you see is what you have.
- Simplicity: This method reduces complexity for those who find accounting daunting, making it easier to manage without specialized knowledge.
- Timing: It can be beneficial for tax purposes. By managing when you pay expenses and receive income, you can strategically influence your taxable income for the year.

However, it's not without limitations. It can obscure the proper financial health of your business by ignoring pending obligations and expected receipts. If your business extends credit to customers or carries significant inventory, the cash method may offer a misleading picture of financial stability.

Exploring "Accrual Basis" Accounting

Switching gears to accrual-based accounting introduces a method where transactions are recorded when they are earned or incurred, regardless of when cash changes hands. This method offers:

- Accuracy: It provides a more precise picture of your business's financial health, incorporating all liabilities and assets, not just those involving cash transactions.
- Forecasting: With a comprehensive view of finances, planning for the future becomes more reliable. You can anticipate expenses and income better, even if they haven't yet affected your cash position.
- Compliance: As businesses grow, they might be required by law to adopt this method. It's generally accepted

accounting principles (GAAP) compliant, making it necessary for businesses with a specific size or structure.

Accrual accounting can be more complex to implement and maintain. It requires a meticulous approach to tracking payables and receivables, demanding more time and possibly more sophisticated accounting software or expertise.

Making the Right Choice

Deciding on the best method hinges on several factors:

- Business Size and Complexity: Small operations with straightforward transactions lean towards a cash basis for their simplicity. Businesses with inventory, credit sales, or those that exceed revenue thresholds set by tax authorities might benefit from or be required to use accrual accounting.
- Cash Flow: If managing cash flow is a priority, starting with the cash method provides direct insight into cash availability.
- Tax Considerations: Cash-based accounting can offer flexibility in managing taxable income, but consulting with a tax advisor is wise to understand the implications fully.
- Future Needs: Consider where your business is now and where it's headed. Switching accounting methods later can be a complex process requiring adjustments to ensure past transactions align with the new method.

Switching Between Methods

There might come a time when shifting from cash to accrual accounting (or vice versa) aligns better with your business's evolving needs. This transition is not as simple as flipping a switch; it requires recalibrating your financial records to reflect income and expenses according to the new method. For instance, switching to accrual means recognizing receivables and payables not previously recorded under cash accounting. It's a process that often benefits from professional guidance to ensure compliance and accuracy.

Your choice of accounting method lays the foundation for tracking, managing, and planning your business finances. It influences everything from day-to-day bookkeeping to strategic decision-making and compliance. As such, it warrants careful consideration, balancing the need for simplicity and clarity against the desire for a comprehensive view of your financial health.

2.2 ESSENTIAL BOOKKEEPING TOOLS: SOFTWARE AND MANUAL OPTIONS REVIEWED

In small business finance, the tools you employ can significantly influence the efficiency and accuracy of your bookkeeping practices. This section explores the nuances of choosing between modern software solutions and traditional manual bookkeeping methods, providing insights to inform decision-making.

Evaluating Bookkeeping Software

Navigating the landscape of bookkeeping software requires a keen eye for features that align with your business's specific needs. Considerations include:

- Features: Look for software that offers a range of functionalities beyond basic ledger entries, such as invoicing, expense tracking, and financial reporting. The goal is to find a system that records transactions and offers insights into your financial health.

- Ease of Use: The interface should be intuitive, minimizing the learning curve for you and your team. A user-friendly platform ensures you can quickly access and understand your financial data without extensive training.
- Scalability: Your business is not static, and your bookkeeping software shouldn't be either. Opt for solutions that can grow with your business, accommodating increased transaction volumes and additional users without a hitch.
- Integration Capabilities: In today's interconnected digital world, the ability to seamlessly integrate with other business tools, such as payroll services, customer relationship management (CRM) systems, and e-commerce platforms, is invaluable. This connectivity ensures a cohesive flow of information across different facets of your business.
- Security: Financial data is sensitive, and the software must offer robust security measures, including encryption and multi-factor authentication, to protect against unauthorized access and data breaches.

Considering Manual Bookkeeping

While digital solutions dominate the conversation, manual bookkeeping remains a viable option for some small businesses. This approach involves physical ledgers or electronic spreadsheets and requires a meticulous hand. Benefits and drawbacks include:

- Cost Efficiency: Manual bookkeeping can be more cost-effective for businesses on a tight budget, eliminating the need for subscription fees associated with software solutions.

- Customization: A spreadsheet or paper ledger can be customized to your specific needs without the constraints sometimes imposed by software templates.
- Simplicity: Manual bookkeeping can be straightforward for businesses with minimal transactions, offering a no-frills approach to financial tracking.

However, this method also presents challenges:

- **Time Consumption:** Manual entry of transactions is labor-intensive, potentially diverting valuable time from other business activities.
- **Error Risk:** The likelihood of making calculation errors increases without the automated checks and balances provided by the software.
- **Limited Insights:** Manually generating reports and analyzing data can be cumbersome, potentially hindering your ability to make informed financial decisions.

Integrating with Other Business Tools

The complementary relationship between your bookkeeping system and other business applications is pivotal in streamlining operations. For instance:

- Payroll Integration: Automating the transfer of payroll data into your bookkeeping system saves time and reduces the risk of errors, ensuring that employee compensation is accurately reflected in your financial records.
- E-commerce Platforms: For businesses that sell online, integration between your e-commerce platform and

bookkeeping software automates the recording of sales transactions, inventory changes, and associated fees, providing real-time visibility into your financial performance.

- Payment Processing: Linking your payment processing system directly to your bookkeeping tool simplifies sales and expense tracking, offering a consolidated view of cash flow.

This level of integration enhances efficiency and provides a holistic view of your business's financial activities, enabling more strategic decision-making.

Cost vs. Benefit Analysis

Selecting the right bookkeeping tools involves a cost-benefit analysis, weighing the financial investment against the value delivered to your business. Consider:

- Immediate and Long-Term Costs: Beyond the initial purchase or subscription fee, consider additional costs such as training, customization, or upgrades. Manual bookkeeping, while less expensive upfront, may incur higher long-term costs in terms of time and potential errors.
- Efficiency Gains: Evaluate how much time the tool can save you and your team. Time is a valuable commodity in small business management, and tools that free up hours for strategic activities can be worth the investment.
- Data Accuracy and Insights: Maintaining accurate records and glean actionable insights from your financial data can drive better business outcomes. Tools that enhance these aspects offer significant value.

- Scalability: Assess whether the tool can adapt to your business's growth, ensuring that you won't need to switch systems as your needs evolve, which can be disruptive and costly.

In conclusion, choosing between bookkeeping software and manual methods is not one-size-fits-all. It hinges on understanding your business's unique needs, resources, and goals. By carefully evaluating the options, you can select a tool that keeps your books in order and empowers you to make informed decisions, driving your business toward greater success.

2.3 SETTING UP YOUR CHART OF ACCOUNTS: A STEP-BY-STEP GUIDE

The backbone of any robust bookkeeping system lies in its Chart of Accounts (CoA). This vital component categorizes every financial transaction your business undertakes into distinct accounts, facilitating orderly record-keeping and insightful financial reporting. Here's how to set up a Chart of Accounts that mirrors the unique financial landscape of your business.

Defining "Chart of Accounts"

The Chart of Accounts is a structured list of all ledger account titles and numbers that a business uses to organize its financial transactions. Picture it as the filing system where every financial transaction finds its home, categorized neatly to offer a bird's eye view of your business's finances. This clarity is crucial for daily bookkeeping tasks and drawing up financial statements that provide insights into your business's performance.

Designing Your Chart of Accounts

Crafting a Chart of Accounts tailored to your business involves several thoughtful steps. Begin by considering the nature of your business operations, the complexity of your financial transactions, and your reporting needs. A well-designed Chart of Accounts should:

- Reflect on the unique aspects of your business, acknowledging the diversity of your revenue sources, expenses, assets, and liabilities.
- Anticipate future growth, allowing room to add new accounts as your business evolves.
- Align with standard financial reporting frameworks to streamline tax preparation and compliance.

Start with broad categories for assets, liabilities, equity, revenues, and expenses, then drill down into sub-categories specific to your business. For example, under expenses, you might have accounts for advertising, rent, utilities, and payroll.

Chart of Accounts Example

Chart of Accounts

Assets
    Checking Account
    Savings Account
    Petty Cash
    Accounts Receivable (money owed to you)

Liabilities
    Accounts Payable (money you owe)
    Credit Card
    Bank Loan

Equity
    Common Stock (your ownership)

Income
    Sales

Expenses
    Bank Charges
    Charitable Donations
    Dues/Subscriptions/Licenses
    Insurance
    Interest (Long-term)
    Meals and Entertainment
    Office Expenses
    Professional Fees
    Rent
    Repair and Maintenance
    Supplies
    Taxes
    Travel
    Utilities

Account Types Explained

Navigating the different types of accounts is vital in setting up your Chart of Accounts. Here's a primer on these fundamental categories:

- Assets: These accounts track what your business owns. They range from current assets like cash and inventory, expected to be converted into cash within a year, to fixed assets like buildings and equipment, which are long-term in nature.
- Liabilities: Liabilities accounts record what your business owes to others, including current liabilities, such as accounts payable and short-term loans due within a year, and long-term liabilities, like mortgages payable.
- Equity: This category reflects the owner's or shareholders' stake in the business. It includes retained earnings and any contributions made by the owners.
- Revenues: Revenues accounts capture the income your business generates from its operations, such as sales revenue, service income, or interest revenue.
- Expenses: These accounts show the money spent in earning revenue. This broad category encompasses everything from the cost of goods sold to administrative expenses.

Understanding these account types is critical as they form the structure upon which your entire bookkeeping system is built. Each transaction your business conducts will interact with these accounts, shaping the financial narrative of your enterprise.

Best Practices for Maintenance

Keeping your Chart of Accounts organized and up-to-date is not a one-time task but an ongoing process. Adherence to a few best practices can ensure your Chart of Accounts remains a reliable tool for financial management:

- Regularly Review and Clean Up: As your business grows and changes, so will your financial transactions. Schedule periodic reviews of your Chart of Accounts to retire inactive accounts, add new ones as needed, and ensure that all transactions are categorized correctly.
- Consistency in Use: Ensure consistent recording of transactions in the correct accounts. This consistency is key to maintaining accurate financial records and meaningful financial analysis.
- Limit the Number of Accounts: While creating a new account for every new type of transaction might be tempting, this can lead to an unwieldy and cluttered Chart of Accounts. Instead, aim for a balance that captures the necessary detail without becoming overly complicated.
- Leverage Sub-Accounts: Consider using sub-accounts without cluttering your Chart of Accounts for greater granularity. These can provide detailed insights, such as breaking your expenses into finer categories while still rolling into a primary "Expenses" account.

Setting up your Chart of Accounts is like laying the foundation for a building. It requires careful planning and consideration of your current needs and future goals. By designing a Chart of Accounts that accurately reflects your business's financial transactions and structure, you equip yourself with a powerful tool for monitoring your business's financial health and making informed decisions.

Remember, a well-organized Chart of Accounts simplifies your bookkeeping process and enhances the clarity and utility of your financial reports, serving as a beacon that guides your business toward financial success.

2.4 THE FIRST MONTH: KICKSTARTING YOUR BOOKKEEPING ROUTINE

The initial month of managing your bookkeeping is filled with opportunities to establish a solid groundwork for your financial management. It's crucial to approach this phase with purpose and clarity, setting up a routine that will streamline your financial tracking and reporting processes.

Setting Up a Routine

Creating a structured routine is key for maintaining up-to-date financial records. By segmenting bookkeeping tasks into daily, weekly, and monthly activities, you can ensure a comprehensive overview of your business's financial health without becoming overwhelmed. Consider the following distribution of tasks:

- Daily: Allocate time each day for recording transactions. This habit ensures that every financial activity is accounted for promptly, no matter how minor it seems. Daily tasks also include reviewing cash flow to monitor the business's liquidity.
- Weekly: Dedicate a portion of your week to managing invoices and bills, including sending out invoices to clients and processing payments for bills due. Weekly reconciliation of petty cash and reviewing upcoming financial obligations also fall into this category.

- Monthly: Reserve the end of each month for a thorough review of all financial statements, including the income statement, balance sheet, and cash flow statement. It's also a time to reconcile bank statements and review any outstanding accounts receivable or payable.

This routine ensures that financial tasks are manageable and promotes a habit of regular financial oversight, which is crucial for the early detection of potential issues.

Recording Transactions

The cornerstone of any effective bookkeeping system is the accurate and timely recording of transactions. Your business's financial activity, from sales and purchases to expenses and income, should be documented precisely. This process involves:

- Date and Description: Note the date of each transaction and a brief description of its nature.
- Amount: Record the exact amount involved in the transaction.
- Category: Assign the transaction to the appropriate category within your Chart of Accounts.
- Method of Payment: Indicate the method of payment used, whether it's cash, credit, bank transfer, or any other medium.

This meticulous approach not only aids in maintaining accurate financial records but also simplifies the process of financial analysis and reporting.

Reconciling Bank Statements

Reconciliation of bank statements is a critical monthly task that verifies the accuracy of your bookkeeping against bank records. This process involves:

- Matching Transactions: Compare each entry in your bookkeeping system with the corresponding entry on the bank statement. This step ensures every transaction is accounted for and accurately recorded.
- Identifying Discrepancies: Spot any differences between your records and the bank statement. Discrepancies could arise from bank fees, interest payments, or errors in recording transactions.
- Adjusting Records: Make necessary adjustments to rectify any discrepancies found during reconciliation. This might involve correcting errors or accounting for bank fees and interest that were previously not recorded.

Reconciling bank statements ensures the integrity of your financial records and guards against potential fraud and errors.

Reviewing Financial Health

The final task of your monthly bookkeeping routine should be a comprehensive review of your business's financial statements. This process provides valuable insights into your business's financial performance and position. Focus on:

- Income Statement Analysis: Evaluate your revenue streams and expenses to determine profitability. Look for trends, such as increasing costs or fluctuating income that might require strategic adjustments.

- Balance Sheet Review: Examine assets, liabilities, and equity to gauge the overall financial health of your business. Pay special attention to liquidity and current assets' ratio to liabilities.
- Cash Flow Statement: Analyze cash flow from operating, investing, and financing activities. Positive cash flow from operating activities indicates financial health, while reliance on financing activities might signal potential issues.
- Budget Comparison: Compare actual financial performance against your budgeted projections. This comparison can highlight areas where the business is overperforming or underperforming, guiding future budgeting decisions.

This monthly financial review enhances your understanding of your business's financial standing and informs decision-making, helping you navigate your business toward its financial goals.

Establishing and adhering to a structured bookkeeping routine lays the groundwork for effective financial management. This initial month sets the tone for disciplined financial tracking and analysis, fostering a culture of financial mindfulness that will serve your business well into the future. With each transaction recorded, bank statement reconciled, and financial statement reviewed, you're not just keeping books but weaving the financial fabric of your business's success story.

2.5 STREAMLINING YOUR FINANCIAL RECORDS: TIPS FOR EFFICIENT DOCUMENT MANAGEMENT

Managing financial records often becomes challenging in the bustling world of small business and can consume significant time and energy. Yet, the rewards of a well-oiled document management system are myriad, offering not just peace of mind but also a strong foundation for making informed financial decisions. Here's how to fine-tune this aspect of your business, ensuring that your financial records are not just a collection of numbers but a powerful tool for growth and stability.

Organizing Financial Documents

Creating an orderly system for your financial documents is similar to setting up a library where every book has its place and any piece of information can be swiftly located. This system starts with categorizing documents into clearly defined groups, such as receipts, invoices, bank statements, and payroll records. Each category should have a designated filing cabinet or digital folder space. Within these categories, organizing documents by date or transaction type further streamlines retrieval, ensuring you can find what you need with minimal fuss. This level of organization not only aids in keeping your financial house in order and simplifies tasks like tax preparation and financial review.

Going Digital

The digital transformation of your financial records offers a pathway to increased efficiency and security. By scanning and storing documents electronically, you unlock the benefits of easy access, regardless of your physical location, and the ability to share files swiftly with team members or external advisors. Digital records also reduce the risk of physical damage or loss, ensuring that your financial history remains intact. When transitioning to digital, it's essential to choose a format that's universally accessible and maintain a consistent naming convention for your files, enhancing organization and searchability.

Regular Clean-up

Just as a garden requires regular weeding, your financial records need periodic decluttering to remain functional and relevant. Set aside time, whether monthly or quarterly, to review your documents and dispose of those no longer needed, adhering to legal requirements for record retention. This clean-up extends to digital files, where obsolete documents can clutter your storage system and make navigation cumbersome. By keeping your records lean, you ensure that your document management system remains a facilitator, not a hindrance, to financial clarity.

Data Backup and Security

In an era where data is as valuable as currency, protecting your financial records from loss or theft is paramount. Implementing a robust backup strategy involving on-site and off-site copies safeguards your records against technological failures or physical disasters. Cloud storage services offer a convenient solution for off-site backups, providing storage and enhanced security against unauthorized access. Moreover, the encryption of sensitive files and strong, unique passwords add layers of protection, ensuring that your financial data remains confidential and secure.

In sum, meticulous organization, digitization, regular maintenance, and secure backup of your financial documents form the pillars of efficient document management. By embracing these practices, you transform your financial records from a mere compliance requirement into a strategic asset that supports decision-making, fosters transparency and contributes to the overall resilience of your business. As we move forward, remember that the strength of your financial management practices directly impacts your ability to navigate the complex landscape of small business ownership, steering your venture towards its long-term goals.

The intricacies of setting up and maintaining an effective bookkeeping system are challenging and rewarding. Each step builds towards a comprehensive understanding of your business's financial health, from selecting the correct accounting method to organizing and securing your financial records. As we pivot towards the next chapter, remember the critical role of informed financial decisions in driving business growth and stability.

3

EVERYDAY BOOKKEEPING PRACTICES FOR SMALL BUSINESS SUCCESS

Bookkeeping might not come with the thrill of closing a big sale or the buzz of launching a new product but think of it as the backbone of your business's financial health. It's about keeping your business's heart beating, ensuring every dollar in and out is accounted for. This careful attention to detail can transform a mundane task into a powerful tool for financial insight and business growth.

In this chapter, we dive into the daily rituals that keep your financials in check, your cash flow healthy, and your business decisions informed. It's not about reinventing the wheel but about turning seemingly small daily actions into habits that compound over time, leading to significant benefits for your business.

3.1 DAILY BOOKKEEPING CHECKLIST FOR SMALL BUSINESS OWNERS

A daily bookkeeping checklist is your roadmap to financial clarity and control. By sticking to these tasks, you'll ensure your books are always up to date, giving you the accurate financial information you need to make informed decisions.

Prioritizing Daily Entries

Picture your business transactions as the lifeblood flowing through your business each day. Each entry recorded is like a heartbeat, reflecting the vibrant activity of your business. By prioritizing daily entries, you ensure no transaction slips through the cracks, preventing inaccuracies and backlogs that can cloud your financial picture. Whether it's a sale, a purchase, or an expense, recording it on the day it happens keeps your financial records accurate and up-to-date.

- Why: It's about capturing the moment. Today's transactions are fresh in your mind, making it easier to record them accurately.
- How: Set a fixed time each day for bookkeeping. Consistency is key, whether it's first thing in the morning or right before you close shop.

Reviewing Cash Position

Starting your day clearly understanding your available cash gives you a strategic advantage. It's about knowing your financial footing before making any moves. This daily check-up lets you see if you're in a position to cover your immediate expenses, invest in opportunities, or if you need to tighten your belt.

- Why: Cash is king. Knowing your cash position helps you make decisions confidently, from daily operations to strategic moves.
- How: Use your bookkeeping software's dashboard for a quick overview or check your bank balance if you're keeping things simple.

Monitoring Outstanding Invoices

Invoices are promises of future cash flows, but they're only as good as the payment that follows. Keeping a close eye on outstanding invoices helps you manage your cash flow more effectively, ensuring you follow up on overdue payments before they impact your financial health.

- Why: Late payments can strangle your cash flow. Proactively managing invoices keeps the cash moving and your business healthy.
- How: Use a tracking system within your bookkeeping software to alert you to overdue invoices, making follow-ups a breeze.

Categorizing Expenses

Every expense tells a story about your business's operations and priorities. You turn a pile of receipts into actionable financial insights by categorizing your expenses daily. This practice simplifies tax filing and helps you analyze where your money is going, uncovering opportunities to cut costs or invest more in what's driving growth.

- Why: Categorized expenses are like a map showing where your money is taking you. This clarity is crucial for budgeting and strategic planning.

- How: Implement a system for categorizing expenses as you record them. Most bookkeeping software offers customizable categories to tailor to your business's needs.

By incorporating these tasks into your daily routine, you turn bookkeeping from a chore into a powerful habit. It's about building a foundation of financial diligence that supports everything from day-to-day decisions to long-term strategic planning. Remember, the health of your business's finances depends on the details and consistency of your bookkeeping practices.

3.2 RECORDING TRANSACTIONS: A HOW-TO GUIDE FOR NON-ACCOUNTANTS

Navigating the world of bookkeeping might seem like wading through a sea of numbers and terms for many small business owners. Yet, recording transactions doesn't have to feel like decoding a foreign language. Here, we break down this key process into clear, manageable steps, making it approachable for everyone, irrespective of their accounting background.

Simplifying Transaction Recording

Think of each transaction as a story your business tells about its daily operations. Recording these stories doesn't need to be complicated. Here's how to simplify the process:

- Identify the Transaction: Start by determining the nature of the transaction. Is it an income, an expense, a purchase, or a sale? Recognizing this first step sets the stage.

- Determine the Amount: Next, pinpoint the exact amount involved. Precision here is critical for maintaining accurate books.
- Assign a Date: Every transaction should have a corresponding date. This helps in organizing your records chronologically, making tracking easier.
- Choose the Right Account: Select which account this transaction affects within your Chart of Accounts. It could be a revenue account for sales or an expense account for purchases.
- Document the Details: Finally, note any pertinent details accompanying the transaction. It might include the payment method, the vendor or customer involved, or the purpose of the transaction.

By breaking down the recording process into these steps, what once seemed daunting becomes a straightforward task that anyone can manage.

Using Bookkeeping Software

Modern bookkeeping software is a game-changer for small businesses, automating much of the heavy lifting of recording transactions. Choosing the right software involves evaluating options that align with your business size, industry, and specific needs. Opt for a solution that offers scalability, robust support, and integration capabilities with your other tools. We will explore this topic in more detail in a later chapter.

Understanding Double-Entry Bookkeeping

At its core, double-entry bookkeeping is about balance. For every transaction, two entries are made: one to a debit account and another to a credit account. Here's a simplified breakdown:

- Debit Entries: Increase asset or expense accounts or decrease liability or equity accounts. Think of them as the transaction's "source."
- Credit Entries: These increase liability or equity accounts or decrease asset or expense accounts, acting as the transaction's "destination."
- The Rule of Balance: The total amount of debits must always equal the total amount of credits, maintaining a fundamental balance in your books.

Understanding this principle is crucial for accurately recording transactions and reflecting your business's financial health.

Keeping Receipts and Notes

Supporting every entry with the proper documentation is not just good practice; it's necessary, especially when tax season rolls around. Here's why meticulous record-keeping matters:

- Proof of Transaction: Receipts and notes are evidence of the transactions recorded in your books, which are crucial during audits or when verifying entries.
- Tax Documentation: Many expenses can be tax-deductible. Having detailed records supports your claims, potentially saving you money.

- Dispute Resolution: In the event of disputes with suppliers, customers, or even the tax authorities, comprehensive documentation can quickly clarify matters.

Developing a system for organizing and storing these documents, physically or digitally, ensures you always have the needed information. Consider using cloud storage solutions for digital receipts and notes, offering security and accessibility.

By adopting these practices, recording transactions transforms from a daunting task into a manageable part of your daily routine. With the right approach, software, and a commitment to detail, you maintain accurate books and gain valuable insights into your business's financial narrative.

3.3 THE ART OF INVOICING: CREATING EFFICIENT, EFFECTIVE INVOICES

Invoicing might seem straightforward — you're asking for the rightfully earned payment. However, there's an art to crafting invoices that not only prompt timely payments but also reinforce the professionalism and credibility of your business. From the design to the follow-up, every step in the invoicing process is an opportunity to enhance your business operations and customer relationships.

Designing Professional Invoices

A well-designed invoice serves as a reflection of your business's attention to detail and professionalism. It should be clear, concise, and easy to understand, ensuring clients know exactly what they're paying for, how much they owe, and when payment is due. Key elements to include are:

- Your Business Logo and Contact Information: This not only brands your invoice but also provides clients with easy access to your contact details should they have questions.
- Client Information: Clearly state the client's name, address, and other relevant contact information to avoid confusion.
- Invoice Number: A unique invoice number is crucial for tracking and organization for accounting purposes and referencing specific communications transactions.
- Dates: Include the date the invoice is issued and the payment due date. It helps set clear expectations for payment timelines.
- Detailed Breakdown of Services or Products Provided: Itemize the services or products, including descriptions and costs. This transparency helps prevent disputes and builds trust with your clients.
- Total Amount Due: Highlight the total amount owed prominently on the invoice. If applicable, provide details on any taxes, discounts, or additional fees.
- Payment Terms and Instructions: Clearly outline accepted payment methods and any instructions on how to complete the payment. Removing any barriers to timely payment by making the process as straightforward as possible for your clients.

Streamlining the Invoicing Process

Leveraging templates and software can significantly streamline the invoicing process, reducing the time and effort required to create and send invoices. Many bookkeeping and invoicing software platforms offer customizable invoice templates that you can tailor to your business's needs. These tools often include features that allow for:

- Automatic Calculation: Eliminate manual calculations for totals, taxes, and discounts, reducing the risk of errors.
- Recurring Invoicing: For clients with ongoing services, set up recurring invoices that automatically generate and send according to a predetermined schedule.
- Digital Delivery: Email invoices directly from the software, cutting delivery time and enabling easier tracking of sent, received, and opened invoices.

Implementing Follow-Up Procedures

Even with efficient invoicing practices, occasionally, payments can be delayed. Implementing a structured follow-up procedure ensures that these instances are handled promptly and professionally. Consider:

- Automated Reminders: Many invoicing software solutions offer the ability to send automated payment reminders to clients before and after the due date. This gentle nudge can often prompt payment without the need for direct intervention.
- Personalized Follow-Up: A personalized approach may be more effective if payment is overdue. A phone call or a tailored email can help you understand any reasons for the delay and discuss solutions, such as payment plans for clients facing financial difficulties.

Handling Disputed Invoices

Disputes over invoices, while not common, can occur. Handling these situations tactfully and professionally is crucial to maintaining positive client relations. Here are steps to amicably resolve disputed invoices:

- Review the Dispute: Listen to your client's concerns and review the disputed invoice thoroughly. There may have been a misunderstanding or error that can be easily rectified.
- Provide Documentation: If the dispute concerns the nature or quality of the delivered service or product, provide evidence supporting your case, such as contracts, email correspondence, or delivery receipts.
- Negotiate: If the dispute cannot be resolved with documentation alone, be open to negotiation. Finding a compromise that satisfies both parties can often save a business relationship.
- Formal Procedures: Refer to the payment terms outlined in your contract or agreement for disputes that cannot be resolved through negotiation. You may need to consider formal collection procedures as a last resort.

Invoicing, far from being a mere request for payment, is an integral part of your business's operations and client interactions. A thoughtful approach to designing, sending, and following up on invoices not only facilitates smoother cash flow but also reinforces the professionalism and reliability of your services. By implementing these strategies, you ensure invoicing becomes a seamless, efficient aspect of your business, reflecting the high standards you uphold in every facet of your work.

3.4 MANAGING EXPENSES: KEEP YOUR CASH FLOW HEALTHY

In the dynamic landscape of small business operations, vigilance over expenses is pivotal in maintaining a robust cash flow, a necessary condition for sustaining and growing your business. It's about more than just tracking dollars and cents; it's about creating a strategic approach to financial management that anticipates future needs and identifies opportunities for optimization.

Tracking Expenses Religiously

Meticulously documenting every business expense lays the foundation for effective cash flow management. This rigorous approach offers a dual advantage: it ensures that every financial commitment is accounted for and provides a detailed record that can be leveraged for strategic planning and tax preparation. To achieve this, consider implementing a system that:

- Automatically categorizes expenses as they occur, using bookkeeping software to integrate with your bank and credit card accounts for real-time tracking.
- Sets alerts for significant or unusual transactions, allowing for immediate review and adjustment where necessary.

This methodical tracking fosters a proactive stance towards financial management, enabling you to anticipate and address cash flow challenges before they escalate.

Separating Personal and Business Expenses

Blurring the lines between personal and business finances can complicate your financial analysis and tax reporting, potentially leading to inaccuracies that could affect your bottom line. Establishing a clear distinction between these two realms enhances the clarity of your financial records, simplifying tax preparation and supporting more accurate financial forecasting. Strategies to ensure this separation include:

- Opening a dedicated business bank account and credit card used exclusively for business transactions.
- Implementing a reimbursement policy for any personal funds used for business expenses, complete with proper documentation and categorization.

This clarity streamlines your financial processes and fortifies your business's integrity, safeguarding against potential complications during tax season or financial audits.

Negotiating with Suppliers

Your relationships with suppliers can be valuable in optimizing cash flow. Engaging in negotiations to secure more favorable payment terms or discounts for early payment can significantly enhance your cash flow position. Approach these negotiations with a strategy that:

- Involves thorough preparation, understanding your current spending, and the market rates for the goods or services you're purchasing.
- Focuses on building long-term relationships with suppliers, emphasizing mutual benefits and reliability as a customer.
- Consider multiple suppliers to ensure you have bargaining power and alternatives.

By actively managing your supplier relationships, you improve your immediate cash flow and establish a foundation for sustainable financial management practices that can support your business's growth.

Regular Expense Review

The landscape of business expenses is not static; it evolves in response to changes in operations, market conditions, and strategic direction. Regularly reviewing your recurring expenses ensures that your spending aligns with your business needs and goals. This periodic assessment should:

- Identify services or subscriptions that are no longer necessary or replaceable with more cost-effective alternatives.
- Evaluate the ROI of significant expense categories, determining whether they contribute positively to your business objectives.
- Explore opportunities for bulk purchasing or long-term contracts that could offer savings.

This dynamic approach to expense management not only aids in trimming unnecessary costs but also ensures that your spending is strategic, directly contributing to the efficiency and growth of your business.

By embracing these principles, you move beyond expense tracking to strategic financial management. This proactive stance safeguards your cash flow and supports informed decision-making and strategic planning, laying a solid foundation for your business's financial health and success.

3.5 RECONCILING ACCOUNTS: A SIMPLE GUIDE TO KEEPING BOOKS ACCURATE

Keeping your financial records straight is like maintaining a well-tuned engine in your car—it ensures everything runs smoothly and prevents unexpected breakdowns. Regular reconciliation of your accounts plays a crucial role in this process, acting as a routine check-up to catch and correct any discrepancies that might otherwise lead your business astray.

When you reconcile your accounts, you compare your internal financial records against external records (typically your bank statements) to verify that they match. It's a fundamental practice that not only ensures the accuracy of your financial information but also guards against fraud and helps maintain a clear picture of your cash flow.

The Importance of Regular Reconciliation

Imagine sailing a ship without ever checking if you're on course. Without regular reconciliation, navigating the financial waters of your business could lead you off track. This process is vital for several reasons:

- Accuracy of Financial Statements: Regular reconciliation helps ensure that the financial statements you rely on for decision-making accurately reflect your business's financial position.
- Fraud Detection: By routinely comparing your records with bank statements, you can quickly spot unauthorized transactions, giving you a better chance to address any issues swiftly.

- Error Correction: Mistakes happen, but regular reconciliation allows you to catch and correct errors before they compound, ensuring your financial data remains reliable.

Step-by-Step Reconciliation Process

Follow this simple, systematic approach each month to keep your accounts in check:

1. Gather Your Documents: Start by collecting your internal financial records and the corresponding bank statements for the period you're reconciling.
2. Match Transactions: Go through your records and bank statements side by side. Find the matching transaction on the bank statement for each transaction in your records.
3. Check Balances: Once all transactions match, compare the ending balance in your records to the ending balance on the bank statement. They should align. If not, it's time to dig deeper.
4. Identify Discrepancies: Look for transactions in your records but not on the bank statement, and vice versa. Also, watch for differences in transaction amounts.
5. Make Adjustments: Adjust your records to reflect any missed transactions or correct any errors found. You may need to add missing transactions or correct the recorded transaction amounts.

This systematic approach, done regularly, keeps your financial records accurate, giving you confidence in the financial information you use to make business decisions.

Identifying and Correcting Discrepancies

When you find differences between your bookkeeping records and your bank statement, it's crucial to address them promptly. Here's how:

- Investigation: For each discrepancy, go back to the original documents—receipts, invoices, and payment records—to understand the source of the mismatch.
- Correction: If the discrepancy is due to an error in your records, adjust the entry to reflect the correct information. If it's a transaction you missed, add it to your records.
- Documentation: Keep notes on any adjustments made, including the reason for the discrepancy and how it was resolved. This documentation can be invaluable for future reference, especially during audits.

Systematically addressing discrepancies ensures that your financial records accurately represent your business's financial activities, providing a solid foundation for informed decision-making.

Using Software to Simplify Reconciliation

While manual reconciliation is doable, modern bookkeeping software can significantly streamline the process, saving you time and reducing the risk of errors. Many software platforms offer features designed to simplify reconciliation, such as:

- Automatic Transaction Matching: Software can automatically compare transactions in your records to those on your bank statement, highlighting matches and flagging discrepancies.

- Real-Time Data Sync: By connecting your bookkeeping software directly to your bank account, importing transactions can be automatic, ensuring your records are always up to date.
- Discrepancy Alerts: Some platforms will alert you to discrepancies during reconciliation, helping you identify and address issues more quickly.

Leveraging these tools can transform reconciliation from a tedious task into a more manageable and efficient part of your monthly financial routine.

Maintaining accurate books through regular reconciliation is akin to navigating with a reliable compass—ensuring you're always headed in the right direction. By making this process a routine part of your financial management, you safeguard the integrity of your financial information, allowing you to steer your business confidently. As we move forward, remember that each step taken to ensure the accuracy of your financial records is a step towards securing your business's financial health and future success.

4

CASH FLOW MASTERY: NAVIGATING THE EBB AND FLOW

Picture a bustling café on a Monday morning, the aroma of freshly brewed coffee in the air, a line of customers out the door. Now, imagine the café runs out of coffee beans. Surprising, isn't it? This scenario, while simplistic, underscores the essence of cash flow management. It's not solely about having enough money; it's about having cash at the right time. Like a café running out of coffee beans, a business without timely cash flow can find itself in a bind, unable to meet its most basic needs.

4.1 UNDERSTANDING CASH FLOW: THE LIFEBLOOD OF YOUR BUSINESS

Cash flow, the movement of money in and out of your business, is its lifeblood. It's what keeps the lights on, pays the employees, and enables growth. Yet, it's often misunderstood, with many equating profitability with healthy cash flow. This chapter aims to clear the fog around cash flow, exploring its nuances through real-life analogies, actionable strategies, and practical advice.

Defining Cash Flow

Cash flow is the timing and movement of money flowing in and out of your business. It's vital for survival and growth, ensuring you have the funds to pay suppliers, employees, and yourself. A positive cash flow means your business is running smoothly, while a negative cash flow signals trouble on the horizon. It's the difference between a café with enough coffee beans for the Monday morning rush and one without.

Types of Cash Flow

Cash flow is categorized into three types:

- Operational Cash Flow: Money made from your business's core activities. Think of it as the daily income from selling coffee and pastries at the café.
- Investment Cash Flow: This involves money spent on or made from investments, like purchasing a new espresso machine or selling an old piece of equipment.
- Financing Cash Flow: Money from loans, repayments, or shareholder investments. It includes things like getting a loan to open another café location or paying back a loan you took to start the business.

Each type impacts your business's health differently, and understanding these distinctions can help you make more informed financial decisions.

Common Cash Flow Misconceptions

One widespread myth is that a profitable business will always have a healthy cash flow. However, profitability doesn't guarantee immediate cash availability. For example, if your café sells a record number of coffee subscriptions but most customers pay at the end of the month, you might struggle to buy supplies. Another misconception is that cutting costs always improves cash flow. While reducing expenses can help, it's equally important to manage the timing of cash inflows and outflows.

Analyzing Cash Flow Statements

A cash flow statement breaks down how much money is coming into and going out of your business, offering a clear picture of its financial health. Here's how to get started with analyzing one:

1. Start with Operational Cash Flow: Look at the net income and adjust for non-cash items (like depreciation) and changes in working capital. This shows how much cash your day-to-day operations are generating.
2. Examine Investment Cash Flow: This section tells you if your business is investing in its future growth. A negative number here isn't necessarily alarming; it might mean you're investing in long-term assets.
3. Review Financing Cash Flow: Here, you'll see the net flow of funds used to finance your company. A positive number could indicate new loans or investments, while a negative number might show repayments.

Learning to read and interpret your cash flow statement is like reading the weather before sailing out to sea. It helps you anticipate and navigate financial challenges, ensuring your business survives and thrives in the ever-changing business climate.

Mastering cash flow is about more than keeping your business afloat; it's about steering it toward sustained growth and success.

It requires vigilance, understanding, and proactive management. By demystifying cash flow, recognizing its types, debunking common myths, and learning to analyze cash flow statements, you equip yourself with the knowledge to make smarter financial decisions. This chapter serves as your compass, guiding you through the complexities of cash flow management and ensuring you're well-prepared to handle whatever financial currents come your way.

4.2 FORECASTING CASH FLOW: PLANNING FOR THE FUTURE

Forecasting cash flow is similar to sketching a map for a treasure hunt, where the treasure is your business's success and growth. This map doesn't just guide you; it helps you anticipate obstacles and opportunities, ensuring you're well-prepared for whatever lies ahead. The core of cash flow forecasting is about predicting the inflows and outflows of cash to your business over a future period. This foresight is invaluable, enabling you to make informed decisions about investments, expenses, and funding needs well in advance.

The Basics of Cash Flow Forecasting

Initiating cash flow forecasting starts with understanding your current financial standing. It's crucial to consider your historical cash flow patterns, identifying the regular ebbs and flows in your business's finances. These patterns serve as the foundation upon which you'll project future financial movements. Think of it as plotting the known landmarks on your map, providing a basis for charting the unexplored territories.

The primary goal here is to pinpoint future periods of positive cash flow, which signal opportunities for growth investments, and negative cash flow, which might necessitate funding arrangements. Forecasting helps ensure you have enough cash reserves to cover upcoming expenses, preventing potential cash shortages that could stall your operations.

Tools for Forecasting

Several tools can simplify forecasting, ranging from basic spreadsheet templates to sophisticated software solutions. These tools offer varying degrees of complexity and automation:

- Spreadsheets: Excel or Google Sheets can be powerful tools when used correctly. They allow for customizable cash flow projections, accommodating unique business needs. Templates can include formulas that automatically calculate projected cash flow based on inputted assumptions about income and expenses.
- Dedicated Forecasting Software: Several software solutions are designed specifically for cash flow forecasting. These platforms often integrate with your existing accounting software, pulling historical data to automate forecasting. Features might include scenario planning, real-time updates, and predictive analytics, offering a more dynamic and detailed view of your future financial position.

Selecting the right tool depends on your business's complexity, the level of detail required, and the resources available for managing the forecasting process.

Adjusting Forecasts Based on Trends

A static forecast is a map that doesn't account for changing weather conditions. Your cash flow forecast needs regular updates to maintain its relevance. These adjustments are based on both internal performance metrics and external economic indicators:

- Internal Performance Metrics: Keep a close eye on your business's financial performance. Significant deviations from expected revenue or expenses should prompt an immediate forecast update. This might include adjusting for a new client contract or an unexpected increase in material costs.
- External Economic Indicators: Changes in the broader economic landscape can profoundly impact your business's cash flow. Including fluctuating interest rates affecting your borrowing costs and market downturns impacting customer spending. Stay attuned to these external factors, adjusting your forecast to reflect their potential impact on your business.

This dynamic approach ensures your forecast remains a relevant tool, guiding your financial decisions accurately as conditions change.

Scenario Planning

The future is inherently uncertain. Scenario planning allows you to prepare for multiple potential outcomes to navigate this uncertainty. This involves creating several versions of your cash flow forecast, each based on different assumptions about the future:

- Best Case Scenario: This forecast assumes everything goes as well as possible. Sales reach their highest potential, expenses are managed efficiently, and external conditions are favorable. It outlines the optimal growth path if all the stars align.
- Worst Case Scenario: This forecast imagines a situation where challenges mount. Sales fall short, expenses overrun, and economic conditions worsen. It's a stress test for your business, highlighting potential vulnerabilities and funding gaps.
- Most Likely Scenario: This forecast lies between the two extremes, based on the most realistic assumptions about future performance and conditions. It's grounded in the known factors and most probable outcomes, serving as the primary guide for your financial planning.

Engaging in scenario planning equips you with strategies for diverse future states, ensuring you're never caught off guard. It encourages proactive rather than reactive management, enabling you to steer your business confidently through uncertain waters.

Foreseeing the future financial landscape of your business through cash flow forecasting is not about predicting with absolute certainty; it's about preparation and adaptability. It arms you with the knowledge to make strategic decisions and secures you in understanding how those decisions could play out under various future scenarios. This proactive approach to financial planning is crucial for navigating a business's inevitable ups and downs, ensuring you're always moving forward and prepared for the challenges and opportunities ahead.

4.3 STRATEGIES FOR IMPROVING CASH FLOW: PRACTICAL TIPS FOR SMALL BUSINESSES

Navigating the complex waters of business finance often requires a keen eye on cash flow management. It's about ensuring your business has the liquidity to meet its obligations while seizing growth opportunities. Below, we explore several practical strategies to bolster your business's cash flow, ensuring you have the financial flexibility to thrive.

Accelerating Receivables

Prompt payment from customers is crucial for maintaining healthy cash flow. Here are some strategies to encourage quicker payments:

- Digital Payment Solutions: Utilize online payment platforms to make it easier for customers to settle invoices. The convenience of digital transactions can significantly shorten payment cycles.
- Incentivize Early Payments: Consider offering discounts for early payment. Even a small percentage of the total bill can motivate customers to pay sooner rather than later.
- Streamline Invoicing: Ensure invoices are clear, accurate, and sent promptly. An invoice that's easy to understand reduces the likelihood of disputes and delays.
- Regular Follow-ups: Establish a routine for following up on outstanding invoices. A gentle reminder before the due date and subsequent follow-ups: if payment is delayed, keep your invoice top of mind for your customers.

These strategies can ensure your cash inflows remain steady and predictable.

Delaying Payables Wisely

While it's important to manage debts responsibly, strategically managing your payables can free up cash flow. Here's how:

- Negotiate Longer Payment Terms: Speak with suppliers to extend payment deadlines. Many are willing to accommodate for longer terms if it means maintaining a good business relationship.
- Leverage Payment Cycles: Time your payments to maximize liquidity. If a supplier offers a 30-day payment term, use that time to keep cash on hand for other immediate needs.
- Electronic Funds Transfer: Schedule payments through electronic funds transfer to ensure they're made on the last day they are due. This keeps funds in your account for as long as possible without incurring late fees.

These tactics can help maintain a positive supplier relationship while optimizing cash flow.

Managing Inventory Efficiently

Inventory management is a delicate balance; too much inventory ties up cash, while too little can lead to stockouts and lost sales. Here are ways to manage inventory for optimal cash flow:

- Just-in-Time Inventory: Adopt a just-in-time inventory system where materials are ordered and received as needed for production. This approach minimizes the cash tied up in unsold stock.
- Regular Inventory Audits: Conduct frequent audits to identify slow-moving or obsolete items. Consider

discounting these items to free up warehouse space and convert them into cash.

- Dropshipping: For certain products, consider a dropshipping model where items are shipped directly from the supplier to the customer. This eliminates the need to hold inventory altogether.

Efficient inventory management ensures your cash is not unnecessarily tied up in stock, improving liquidity.

Leveraging Financing Options

In certain situations, external financing can boost the necessary cash flow to bridge gaps or seize growth opportunities. Here are some options:

- Lines of Credit: Establishing a line of credit with a bank offers access to funds that can be used as needed and repaid on flexible terms. It's a safety net for when cash flow is tight.
- Factoring: Factoring involves selling your accounts receivable at a discount to a third party. You get immediate cash, and the factoring company takes on the risk of collecting the debt.
- Merchant Cash Advances: For businesses with significant credit card sales, a merchant cash advance provides upfront cash in exchange for a portion of future sales. It's a quick way to access capital, though often at higher costs.
- Trade Credit: Negotiating trade credit with suppliers allows you to receive goods or services upfront with the agreement to pay later. This can free up cash for other immediate needs.

Each financing option comes with its considerations, from cost to repayment terms. Evaluating these carefully is vital to determine the best fit for your business's cash flow needs.

By implementing these strategies, small businesses can proactively manage their cash flow, ensuring they have the liquidity to cover operational costs, take advantage of growth opportunities, and navigate the financial challenges that come their way. It's about taking control of your financial destiny and making strategic decisions that align with your business objectives and cash flow realities.

4.4 DEALING WITH CASH FLOW CHALLENGES: SOLUTIONS FOR COMMON PROBLEMS

Cash flow challenges can arise even in the most prosperous businesses, turning a seemingly smooth sail into a struggle against the current. Recognizing these hurdles early on and addressing them with short-term fixes and long-term strategies ensures your business survives and thrives. Seeking professional advice can also provide the insights needed to navigate these waters efficiently.

Identifying Cash Flow Problems Early

Regular monitoring and analysis of your financial statements play a critical role in the early detection of cash flow problems. This proactive approach allows you to spot warning signs before they escalate into more significant issues. Key indicators include:

- A consistent decrease in cash balance over several periods without a comparable increase in investment or inventory.
- Increasing accounts receivable, signaling that customers are taking longer to pay.

- Rising short-term debt to cover operational costs, indicating reliance on borrowing to maintain liquidity.

Setting up a system for regular financial review, weekly or monthly, lets you avoid potential cash flow problems. Utilizing dashboards and financial management tools that provide real-time data can also aid in this early detection process.

Solving Short-Term Cash Shortages

When faced with immediate cash flow shortages, several strategies can help you bridge the gap without compromising your business operations:

- Cut Unnecessary Expenses: Review your spending to identify areas where costs can be reduced. Temporary measures, such as postponing non-essential purchases or negotiating for lower prices on essential items, can free up cash.
- Access Short-Term Financing: Options such as a line of credit, short-term loans, or even business credit cards can provide the necessary funds to navigate tight spots. Ensure these are used judiciously, with a clear plan for repayment to avoid accumulating debt.
- Invoice Financing: If outstanding invoices are the source of your cash crunch, consider invoice financing to get an advance on the amounts due.

These approaches can provide immediate relief, allowing you more time to implement long-term solutions to stabilize your cash flow.

Strategies for Long-Term Cash Flow Improvement

Focusing on long-term strategies to bolster your cash flow is crucial for sustainable financial health. These include:

- Diversifying Revenue Streams: Don't rely solely on a single product, service, or customer. Explore new markets, introduce complementary products or services, and broaden your customer base to mitigate the risk of income fluctuations.
- Improving Margins: Analyze your pricing strategy and cost structure. Adjusting your prices, even slightly, or reducing production costs can significantly impact your profit margins and, consequently, your cash flow.
- Regularly Reviewing and Adjusting Terms with Suppliers and Customers: Negotiate more favorable payment terms with suppliers, such as extended payment periods, and tighten your payment terms with customers to ensure quicker cash inflows.
- Investing in Efficiency: Automating processes, investing in technology, or training your team can lead to more efficient operations, reducing costs and improving cash flow over the long term.

Implementing these strategies requires a detailed understanding of your business operations and financial metrics. It's a continual adjustment and optimization process, reflecting changes in your business environment and strategy.

Seeking Professional Advice

Complex cash flow challenges sometimes feel like navigating a maze without a map. In such situations, turning to financial professionals can provide clarity and direction. Whether it's an accountant, a financial advisor, or a business consultant, these experts can offer:

- Insightful Analysis: They can objectively analyze your financial situation, identifying underlying issues and offering solutions you might have yet to consider.
- Strategic Planning: Professionals can help you develop a comprehensive financial strategy that addresses immediate cash flow concerns and sets a foundation for long-term financial health.
- Access to Resources and Networks: Financial advisors often have access to a wide range of tools, resources, and contacts that can be invaluable in solving cash flow problems, from financing options to operational efficiency tools.

When choosing a professional to consult with, look for someone with experience in your industry and a track record of solving similar financial challenges. Ensuring they can provide tailored advice that genuinely addresses the specifics of your business.

Facing cash flow challenges is a common part of running a business, but it doesn't have to be a roadblock to success. You can navigate these challenges effectively by staying vigilant, addressing issues promptly with short-term fixes, implementing long-term strategies for improvement, and seeking expert advice when needed. This approach secures your business's presence and paves the way for a financially healthy future, where cash flow problems are no longer a threat but a manageable aspect of your business's growth journey.

4.5 CASH FLOW ANALYSIS: MAKING SENSE OF YOUR CASH FLOW STATEMENTS

In the world of small business, understanding the ebb and flow of finances is like reading a river's current before setting sail. A cash flow statement serves as your navigational chart, offering insights into the financial currents at play within your business. Through this document, you can gauge the strength of your operations, the wisdom of your investments, and the sustainability of your financing strategies.

Breaking Down the Sections of a Cash Flow Statement

At first glance, a cash flow statement might resemble a ledger of incomings and outgoings, yet it tells a far richer story. This statement is divided into three distinct sections(Operational, Investing, and Financing Activities), each reflecting a different aspect of your business's financial activities.

Understanding these components is crucial for interpreting your business's finances' overall health and direction.

Spotting Trends and Patterns

A single cash flow statement offers valuable insights, but analyzing statements over multiple periods reveals patterns and trends vital for strategic planning. By comparing statements side by side, you might notice:

- Seasonal fluctuations in operational cash flow, highlighting periods of high liquidity or potential cash crunches.

- Trends in investing activities include consistent investment in growth or divestment from underperforming assets.
- Changes in financing activities indicate shifts in debt levels or changes in equity financing.

These trends provide a roadmap for future planning, highlighting areas of strength and pinpointing potential vulnerabilities.

Informing Business Decisions

With a deep understanding of your cash flow statement, you can make more informed decisions about your business's future. For example:

- A consistent increase in operational cash flow might signal the right time to expand your operations.
- A trend of significant cash outflows in investing activities could prompt a review of your investment strategy to ensure it aligns with your long-term goals.
- Changes in financing activities might lead you to reassess your debt and equity financing approach, ensuring it supports your business's growth without compromising its financial stability.

In essence, cash flow analysis becomes a tool for understanding where your business stands today and plotting where it can go tomorrow.

Benchmarking Against Industry Standards

To truly understand the significance of your cash flow statement, it helps to place it in the context of broader industry benchmarks.

By comparing your business's cash flow performance against industry averages, you can:

- Identify areas where your business outperforms the competition, highlighting strengths to build upon.
- Spot areas where your business lags, pinpointing opportunities for improvement.
- Gauge your business's competitiveness in the marketplace, informing strategic adjustments to enhance your market position.

This comparison offers a broader perspective on your business's financial health, situating it within the competitive landscape of your industry.

In wrapping up, cash flow analysis emerges as a critical tool for navigating the financial complexities of running a small business. By dissecting your cash flow statement, identifying patterns, leveraging this analysis for strategic decision-making, and comparing your performance against industry benchmarks, you equip yourself with the knowledge to guide your business through calm and turbulent financial waters. This understanding enhances your day-to-day financial management and shapes your strategic vision, setting the stage for sustained growth and success.

As we turn the page, our exploration continues, delving deeper into the financial strategies and practices that can fortify your business's foundations, ensuring its longevity and prosperity in the ever-evolving business landscape.

5

NAVIGATING TAX WATERS WITH
EASE: A SMALL BUSINESS GUIDE

I magine setting sail on the vast ocean without a compass or map, relying solely on the stars for guidance. Now, picture navigating your small business through the complex world of taxes with a similar lack of direction. Both scenarios can lead to unnecessary stress and potential pitfalls. However, with the right knowledge and tools, managing your business taxes becomes less about guesswork and more about strategic planning. This chapter is your compass in the often turbulent tax waters, providing clear, actionable advice to help you steer your small business toward tax compliance and optimization.

5.1 TAX BASICS FOR SMALL BUSINESS OWNERS: WHAT YOU NEED TO KNOW

Understanding Your Tax Obligations

Taxes come in various forms, and understanding which applies to your business is the first step towards compliance. Here's a breakdown:

- Income Tax: Almost every business must file an annual income tax return. The form you use depends on your business structure.
- Sales Tax: If you sell physical products, you'll likely need to collect and remit sales tax. This varies by state and locality.
- Employment Taxes: Have employees? Then you're responsible for taxes like Social Security and Medicare (FICA), Federal Unemployment Tax (FUTA), and withholding taxes.
- Excise Taxes: Specific industries (like alcohol, tobacco, and fuel) are subject to these taxes on certain products.

Each tax has its own rules, rates, and filing deadlines, making it crucial to know which ones apply to your business operations.

Keeping Accurate Records

The importance of meticulous record-keeping can't be overstated when it comes to taxes. Here's what you should keep on file:

- Sales and Income Records: Track all income sources, including sales and services provided.

- Expense Receipts: Keep detailed records of business expenses, from rent and utilities to office supplies and travel.
- Payroll Records: Document all employee compensation, including wages, benefits, and taxes withheld.
- Inventory Records: Maintain inventory purchases and sales records, which can affect your cost of goods sold and overall taxable income.

A best practice is to retain these records for at least three years, during which the IRS can audit your tax returns. However, some documents should be kept longer, especially if they relate to assets or long-term liabilities.

Selecting the Correct Business Structure

Your choice of business structure – sole proprietorship, partnership, LLC, or corporation – has significant tax implications. Here's a quick overview:

- Sole Proprietorships and Partnerships: These structures report business income on personal tax returns, potentially simplifying tax filing and mixing business and personal liabilities.
- LLCs: An LLC offers flexibility, allowing owners to choose between being taxed as a partnership or a corporation, affecting how profits are taxed and distributed.
- Corporations (C and S): C corporations are taxed separately from their owners, while S corporations allow profits and losses to pass through to owners' personal tax returns, avoiding double taxation.

Choosing the right structure for your business can influence your tax rates, filing requirements, and personal liability.

Navigating Estimated Taxes

For many small business owners, paying taxes is not just an annual event but a quarterly obligation. Here's why and how:

- Why Estimated Taxes?: If you expect to owe $1,000 or more in taxes for the year, the IRS requires you to make estimated tax payments throughout the year. This applies to income not subject to withholding, such as earnings from self-employment, interest, dividends, and rent.
- How to Calculate: Estimate your expected adjusted gross income, taxable income, deductions, and credits for the year. Use Form 1040-ES to calculate the amount.
- Payment Schedule: Estimated taxes are typically paid in four installments – April 15, June 15, September 15, and January 15 of the following year.

Failing to make estimated tax payments can result in penalties and interest charges, so planning these payments as part of your annual tax strategy is crucial.

By understanding your tax obligations, maintaining accurate records, choosing the appropriate business structure, and managing estimated taxes, you can confidently navigate the complexities of small business taxation. This proactive approach helps ensure compliance and positions your business to take advantage of potential tax benefits and optimizations. Remember, when it comes to taxes, being well-prepared means being well-armed to make the best decisions for your small business's financial health.

5.2 PLANNING FOR TAX SEASON: A YEAR-ROUND APPROACH

Taxes, often seen as a once-a-year ordeal, actually weave through the daily fabric of your business operations. Transforming tax preparation from a frantic scramble to a strategic year-long endeavor not only eases the burden when filing season approaches but can also significantly impact your business's financial health. Here's how you can shift gears and treat tax planning as an integral part of your ongoing business strategy.

Staying Organized Year-Round

Maintaining orderly records and documentation throughout the year is the secret to a stress-free tax season. Implementing a system that seamlessly integrates tax documentation into your daily routine ensures that you're not wading through a year's worth of paperwork during tax time. Consider these strategies:

- Adopt digital tools and software designed for small business accounting. Many offer features that categorize expenses, track sales, and even flag tax-deductible transactions as they happen.
- Schedule monthly reviews of your financial records. This keeps your accounting up to date and allows you to adjust tax strategies in real-time based on your business's financial performance.
- Use cloud storage solutions to keep digital copies of receipts, invoices, and other tax documents. To prevent data loss or breaches, ensure these are backed up and securely encrypted.

Utilizing Tax Planning Services

While software and digital tools offer considerable help, the expertise of a tax professional can be invaluable, especially when it comes to strategic tax planning. A tax advisor can:

- Provide insights into tax-saving opportunities specific to your industry and business structure.
- Offer guidance on how to structure transactions and timing to optimize tax outcomes.
- Help you understand complex tax laws and how they apply to your business, ensuring you remain compliant while minimizing liability.

Regular consultations with a tax advisor can turn taxes from a liability into an opportunity, helping you leverage tax rules to your business's advantage.

Tax Deduction Strategies

Effective tax planning involves more than just keeping good records; it's about understanding how to strategically time expenses and income to maximize deductions and credits. For instance:

- Accelerating expenses or deferring income can lower taxable income for the current year, providing immediate cash flow benefits.
- Investing in equipment or technology at the end of the fiscal year can offer deductions through depreciation, improving your financial position.

- Taking advantage of tax credits for activities like research and development or green initiatives can significantly reduce tax bills.

Mapping out these strategies requires a good understanding of tax laws and regulations, reinforcing the value of professional tax advice in planning and executing these tactics.

Preparing for Year-End Tax Moves

As the year draws to a close, several strategic moves can help minimize your tax liability while setting your business up for success in the coming year:

- Conduct an inventory assessment. Write down any obsolete or unsellable stock that can be deducted.
- Review outstanding invoices. Consider whether accelerating income or deferring it to the next year would be more advantageous tax-wise.
- Maximize retirement contributions. Contributions to retirement plans can reduce your taxable income, offering both immediate tax benefits and long-term financial security.
- Evaluate your business structure. The end of the year is an excellent time to assess whether a change in your business structure could offer better tax outcomes for the following year.

Treating tax planning as a year-round activity will ease the pressure when tax season rolls around and open up opportunities to significantly improve your business's financial health. This proactive approach allows you to make informed decisions, take timely actions, and steer your business toward greater prosperity.

5.3 MAXIMIZING DEDUCTIONS: TIPS AND STRATEGIES

Navigating the tax landscape requires an understanding of what you owe and an awareness of opportunities to reduce your taxable income. One effective way to manage your tax obligations is by maximizing deductions. Deductions can significantly lower the amount of taxable income, effectively reducing your overall tax burden. Below, explore various deductions your small business might be eligible for and strategies to ensure you're leveraging them to their fullest potential.

Identifying Eligible Deductions

Deductions come in many forms, and knowing what's available can save your business a substantial amount in taxes. Some commonly overlooked deductions include:

- Office Supplies and Equipment: Expenses for items necessary to your business operations, such as computers, printers, and software, can often be deducted.
- Education and Training: Costs associated with training or education that improves your or your employees' skills relevant to your business are deductible.
- Business Insurance: Premiums for business liability, property, and even employee health insurance could be deductible.
- Marketing and Advertising: Money spent on promoting your business, including website development and print or digital advertisements, usually qualifies for a deduction.
- Legal and Professional Fees: Fees paid for legal, accounting, or other professional services directly related to operating your business are often deductible.

- Utilities: Costs for utilities such as electricity, water, and internet service, when used for business purposes, can be deductible.

It's essential to review the IRS guidelines or consult with a tax professional to understand the specific requirements and limits for each type of deduction.

Keeping Good Records

Meticulous record-keeping is the key to maximizing deductions without inviting scrutiny from the IRS. You should have corresponding documentation verifying the expense for every deduction claimed. This could include:

- Receipts: Keep all receipts for purchases and services in your business operations.
- Invoices and Bills: Maintain copies of invoices and bills that detail the services provided, to whom, and the cost.
- Logs and Diaries: For expenses that require more explanation, such as vehicle use for business purposes, keep detailed logs of dates, mileage, and purposes of trips.
- Bank and Credit Card Statements: These can serve as additional proof of purchase for expenses charged to your business accounts.

Digitizing these documents can make storing, organizing, and retrieving them easier, especially if you use accounting software that allows you to attach digital copies of receipts to transactions.

Home Office Deduction

For many small business owners, the home office deduction is a valuable way to reduce taxable income. To qualify, you must use part of your home regularly and exclusively for business. The deduction can be calculated using two methods:

- Simplified Option: Multiply the square footage of your home used for business (up to 300 square feet) by a prescribed rate ($5 per square foot for 2023).
- Regular Method: Calculate the deduction based on the percentage of your home used for business purposes, applying that percentage to direct business expenses and indirect home expenses like mortgage interest, insurance, utilities, and depreciation.

Documenting the use of your home for business, including photos and measurements, can help substantiate your claim for this deduction.

Vehicle and Travel Expenses

Expenses related to business travel, including vehicle use, can also provide significant deductions. To take full advantage:

- Track Business Mileage: Keep a log of miles driven for business purposes. You can deduct a standard mileage rate (58.5 cents per mile for 2023) or actual vehicle expenses (gas, maintenance, depreciation) proportionate to the business use of the vehicle.
- Separate Personal and Business Travel: Only travel expenses directly related to your business are deductible. This includes airfare, lodging, and meals during business

trips. Mixing personal and business travel can complicate deductions, so keep clear records of the business purpose for each trip.

Implementing these strategies to identify and document eligible deductions can significantly reduce your small business's taxable income, leading to substantial tax savings. Staying organized, keeping accurate records, and understanding the nuances of each deduction category will ensure that you're not leaving money on the table come tax time.

5.4 AVOIDING COMMON TAX PITFALLS: HOW TO STAY COMPLIANT

Navigating the tax landscape requires a keen understanding of the rules and regulations that govern small business taxation. Missteps in this arena can lead to unnecessary penalties, interest, and increased scrutiny from tax authorities. This section sheds light on some frequent tax pitfalls and offers guidance on avoiding them, ensuring your business remains in good standing.

Misclassifying Employees and Contractors

The line between employees and independent contractors is more than just a matter of terminology; it has significant tax implications. Here's a closer look:

- Employees typically work under your direction, use your tools and resources, and adhere to your schedule. For these individuals, you must withhold income taxes, withhold and pay Social Security and Medicare taxes, and pay unemployment tax on wages.

- Independent Contractors, on the other hand, operate under their own schedule, use their tools, and work towards delivering a specific result. For these workers, you're not required to withhold or pay taxes; instead, they manage their tax obligations.

The IRS pays close attention to this distinction because misclassifying an employee as an independent contractor can result in failing to pay employment taxes, leading to penalties. To avoid this, carefully review the IRS guidelines on worker classification and apply them when hiring or contracting.

Failing to Report All Income

Every dollar your business earns, whether through sales, services, or passive income streams, must be reported to the IRS. This includes cash transactions, which are often overlooked. Here's why full disclosure matters:

- Reporting only some income can lead to underreporting penalties. To identify discrepancies, the IRS has mechanisms in place, such as comparing your reported income against credit card and bank statements.
- Implement a reliable bookkeeping system that captures every transaction to ensure all income is reported accurately. Regularly reconcile your books with bank statements and other financial records to catch and correct any discrepancies before they become issues.

Embrace transparency in your income reporting to maintain a clean slate with tax authorities and avoid the pitfalls of underreporting.

Not Taking Advantage of All Deductions

Tax deductions benefit small businesses, potentially saving considerable amounts in tax liabilities. However, the fear of triggering an audit deters business owners from claiming legitimate deductions. Here's how to confidently claim what's yours:

- Understand that deductions are there to be used. If you have legitimate business expenses, you have every right to deduct them. The key is ensuring clear, detailed records to back up every claim.
- Educate yourself on what deductions are available and applicable to your business. From home office expenses to vehicle use for business purposes, numerous deductions can reduce your taxable income.
- Use digital tools or consult a tax professional to identify all potential deductions. This maximizes your savings and ensures you're compliant with tax laws.

Claiming all applicable deductions is not about gaming the system; it's about wisely managing your tax obligations. You can take full advantage of these opportunities with thorough documentation and a clear understanding of tax laws.

Avoiding Late Payments and Filing

Timeliness is crucial in tax compliance. Late filings and payments can result in penalties and interest charges, compounding your tax liabilities. Here's how to stay on track:

- Set Reminders: Leveraging digital calendars to set reminders for tax deadlines can help ensure you never miss a date. Consider setting multiple reminders leading up to the deadline for both preparation and submission.

- Implement Systems: Use accounting software that integrates tax planning and preparation features. Many platforms can automatically calculate estimated taxes and remind you when payments are due.
- Plan for Payments: Allocate funds for tax payments well in advance. Setting aside a portion of your income in a separate account for tax purposes can prevent the scramble to find funds when taxes are due.

Staying proactive with your tax filings and payments avoids penalties and instills discipline in your financial management, contributing to your business's overall health and credibility.

By being mindful of these common pitfalls and implementing strategies to avoid them, you can confidently navigate the tax landscape. Proper classification of workers, full income reporting, taking advantage of all deductions, and punctuality in filings and payments form the pillars of tax compliance for small businesses. Upholding these principles ensures that your business stays compliant with tax laws and leverages opportunities to minimize its tax burden.

5.5 HANDLING AUDITS: PREPARING YOUR BUSINESS AND REDUCING STRESS

The word "audit" can trigger a wave of unease for many small business owners. However, with a clear understanding of the process and proper preparation, facing an audit can be more of a calm sea than a turbulent storm. Here, we'll shed light on the audit process, helping you confidently navigate it.

Understanding the Audit Process

Audits are reviews conducted by tax authorities to ensure information on tax returns is reported accurately and to verify that the reported amounts comply with tax laws. Businesses might be selected for an audit for various reasons, including random selection, discrepancies in tax returns, or as part of a targeted check on specific business sectors. During an audit, expect a thorough examination of your financial records, tax returns, and other related documents for a particular tax year.

Preparing Documentation

Being well-prepared with all necessary documentation can significantly streamline the audit process. Here's a checklist to get you started:

- Financial Statements: Ensure you have your balance sheet, income statement, and cash flow statement ready for the period under review.
- Tax Returns: Have copies of the tax returns in question, along with those for years immediately before and after, if available.
- Supporting Documents for Deductions: Gather all receipts, invoices, bank and credit card statements, and any other documents that support the deductions you claimed.
- Records of Business Expenses: Compile logs of business expenses, including travel expenses, office supplies, and any other costs incurred.
- Employment Records: If applicable, prepare payroll records, including wages, taxes withheld, and benefits provided to employees.

Organizing these documents in advance can help make the audit process smoother and more efficient.

Rights and Responsibilities

Knowing your rights and responsibilities during an audit can empower you to engage in the process proactively. Key points include:

- Right to Representation: You have the right to have an accountant, attorney, or other tax professional represent you during the audit. Representation can be beneficial for navigating complex tax issues.
- Right to Privacy and Courtesy: Expect professional and respectful treatment from auditors. They are required to explain the reason for the audit, the scope, and the expected duration.
- Responsibility to Provide Information: You're expected to provide access to the financial records and documents requested by the auditor. Being cooperative can help expedite the audit process.

Understanding these rights and responsibilities ensures a balanced dynamic between you and the auditing body, fostering a cooperative environment.

Reducing Audit Anxiety

The prospect of an audit can be daunting, but several strategies can help mitigate stress and anxiety:

- Stay Organized: Keeping your financial records well-organized year-round means you're already one step ahead. This organization can reduce anxiety by making document retrieval during an audit quick and straightforward.

- Maintain Perspective: Remember, an audit is not an accusation of wrongdoing. It's a standard procedure to verify tax compliance. Keeping this perspective can help alleviate stress.
- Seek Support: Don't hesitate to seek assistance from a tax professional. Their expertise can provide reassurance and reduce the burden of facing the audit alone.
- Practice Self-Care: Recognize that running a business is inherently challenging. Allow yourself breaks and moments of relaxation to maintain your well-being throughout the audit process.

Approaching an audit with preparation and a calm mindset transforms what could be a stressful experience into a manageable and constructive process. It's about having confidence in the accuracy of your financial records and the legitimacy of your tax filings, backed by a thorough understanding of the audit process and your rights within it.

As we wrap up this exploration of tax preparedness and compliance, it's clear that the key to navigating these responsibilities lies in diligent record-keeping, a deep understanding of applicable tax laws, and maintaining a proactive stance towards financial management. This approach positions your business well for tax season and builds a solid foundation for overall financial health and resilience. Moving forward, we'll focus on leveraging financial insights for strategic decision-making, ensuring your business survives and thrives in the competitive marketplace.

Make a Difference with Your Review

Unlock the Power of Generosity

"The smallest act of kindness is worth more than the grandest intention." - Oscar Wilde

Imagine being a superhero without a cape, flying around and spreading joy and success without expecting anything in return. That's what you can be for someone today.

Think about it. Could you be the hero a budding entrepreneur needs? The answer is a resounding yes.

It's true; many folks judge a book by its cover (and what people say about it). So, on behalf of the many small business owners out there who haven't met their mentor yet, I have a small favor to ask:

Could you be that mentor from afar and leave a review for this book?

This no-cost act of kindness takes less than a minute but could forever change the life of another small business owner.

Just scan the QR code below to share your thoughts:

[https://www.amazon.com/review/review-your-purchases/?asin=BOOKASIN]

I can't wait to help you simplify your finances, boost your business's bottom line, and navigate tax season with ease. The tricks up my sleeve in the next chapters will surprise you.

A huge thank you from me to you. Now, let's dive back into the adventure.

6

PAYROLL SIMPLIFIED: A PRACTICAL GUIDE FOR SMALL BUSINESS OWNERS

I magine a world where managing payroll is as straightforward as baking your favorite recipe. You gather the right ingredients (your employee details), follow a step-by-step process (calculating wages and taxes), and, voila, you've created something everyone appreciates on time (payday). This chapter aims to transform the often-overwhelming task of setting up and managing payroll into a clear, manageable process. Let's dive into the essentials of payroll, breaking it down into digestible parts to help you confidently manage this crucial aspect of your business.

6.1 SETTING UP PAYROLL: A STEP-BY-STEP GUIDE FOR THE FIRST-TIME EMPLOYER

Choosing a Payroll System

Selecting the right payroll system is like choosing the best oven for your bakery; it can significantly affect the outcome. Here are the options:

- Manual Processes: Think old-school with paper timesheets and manual calculations. It's cost-effective for small teams but time-consuming and prone to human error.
- Software Solutions: Payroll software automates calculations, tax withholdings, and direct deposits. While there's a cost, the time saved and error reduction can be worth the investment.
- Full-Service Payroll Providers: These services handle everything for you, from calculating pay and deductions to filing taxes. It is ideal for businesses looking to offload payroll tasks entirely.

When deciding, consider your business size, budget, and how much time you can dedicate to payroll tasks. A mix of simplicity and efficiency is usually the goal.

Understanding Legal Obligations

Navigating the legal landscape of payroll involves several key responsibilities:

- Withholding Taxes: You must withhold the correct amount of taxes from employees' paychecks, including federal income tax, Social Security, and Medicare.
- Reporting New Hires: Government agencies require you to report new hires within a specific timeframe. Helping to manage unemployment benefits and child support obligations.
- Complying with Labor Laws: Familiarize yourself with minimum wage laws, overtime requirements, and other labor regulations to ensure compliance.

Staying informed and compliant keeps your business on the right side of the law and builds trust with your team.

Setting Up Employee Records

Accurate employee records are the foundation of a smooth payroll process. Here's a checklist for setting up each employee:

- Personal Information: Full name, address, Social Security number, and contact details.
- Tax Withholdings: Based on each employee's W-4 form, detailing their withholding allowances.
- Employment Agreements: Document the terms of employment, including salary or hourly rate, benefits, and job responsibilities.
- Bank Details: This is for setting up direct deposits.

Having this information organized and accessible simplifies the payroll process and helps address any questions or concerns.

Processing Payroll

The actual process of running payroll involves several steps, ensuring employees are paid correctly and on time. Here's a walk-through:

1. Calculate Gross Pay: For hourly employees, multiply the hours worked by their hourly rate. Divide the annual salary by the number of pay periods for salaried employees.
2. Deduct Withholdings and Taxes: Subtract federal and state taxes, Social Security, and Medicare based on each

employee's tax information. Don't forget deductions for benefits like health insurance or retirement plans.

3. Calculate Net Pay: The employee's take-home pay remains to be issued via check or direct deposit.
4. File Payroll Reports: Regularly submit payroll reports to the appropriate government agencies detailing wages paid and taxes withheld.
5. Maintain Records: Keep detailed records of each payroll cycle, including gross pay, deductions, and net pay for each employee.

While the process might seem daunting initially, breaking it down into these steps makes it more approachable. Plus, most payroll software can automate these tasks, further streamlining the process.

As you set up and manage your payroll, remember that this is more than just a business operation; it's a direct way you support and value your team. By ensuring a smooth, reliable payroll process, you comply with legal obligations and build a solid foundation of trust and reliability with your employees. This, in turn, contributes to a positive work environment and drives the overall success of your business.

6.2 UNDERSTANDING PAYROLL TAXES: WHAT YOU ARE RESPONSIBLE FOR

Navigating the terrain of payroll taxes can feel like decoding a complex map, but once you understand the landmarks, the path becomes clear. Payroll taxes are vital to operating your business, ensuring you and your employees contribute to the broader social safety nets and services the government provides. Here, we break down the components of payroll taxes into understandable segments, ensuring you can confidently manage these obligations.

Federal and State Taxes

The responsibility for withholding federal and state income taxes from employees' paychecks is critical. Each employee's tax situation is unique, influenced by their earnings, filing status, and allowances claimed on their W-4 form. For federal taxes, you'll use the information on the W-4 form and the IRS withholding tables to calculate the correct amount to withhold from each paycheck.

State income taxes follow a similar process, though the specifics can vary widely from one state to another. Some states have a flat tax rate for all residents, while others use a bracket system similar to the federal government. However, A few states do not require state income tax. It's essential to familiarize yourself with the regulations in your state to ensure accurate withholding.

Social Security and Medicare Taxes (FICA)

The Federal Insurance Contributions Act (FICA) mandates the collection of Social Security and Medicare taxes, which are shared responsibilities between you and your employees. Here's how it breaks down:

- Social Security Taxes: You withhold 6.2% of an employee's wages for Social Security and match that amount as the employer. There's an annual wage limit beyond which no Social Security tax is collected.
- Medicare Taxes: Similarly, 1.45% of all wages are withheld for Medicare, with an employer match. Unlike Social Security, there's no wage limit for Medicare taxes.

Additionally, an Additional Medicare Tax of 0.9% may apply for employees earning above a certain threshold, which does not require a matching employer contribution.

Managing FICA taxes requires attention to detail and up-to-date knowledge of the current rates and wage limits.

Unemployment Taxes

Unemployment taxes fund temporary support for workers who have lost their jobs. These taxes include:

- Federal Unemployment Tax Act (FUTA): As an employer, you're responsible for paying FUTA taxes, which are not withheld from employees' wages. FUTA taxes are calculated as a percentage of the first $7,000 paid to each employee annually.
- State Unemployment Taxes: States also levy unemployment taxes, with rates and wage bases varying by location. In many cases, paying state unemployment taxes on time and in full can qualify you for a credit against FUTA taxes.

Understanding the interplay between FUTA and state unemployment taxes can help you effectively manage this aspect of your payroll taxes.

Staying Compliant with Payroll Taxes

Staying on top of your payroll tax obligations ensures your business remains compliant and avoids penalties. Here are some strategies to keep you aligned:

- Leverage Payroll Software: Modern payroll software can automate much of the tax calculation and payment process, reducing the risk of errors and late payments. These systems can keep track of changing tax rates, wage limits, and filing deadlines, making it easier to manage your responsibilities.
- Stay Informed About Tax Rate Changes: Tax rates and wage limits can change yearly. Regularly check for IRS and state tax agency updates to ensure your withholdings and payments are accurate.
- Regular Reviews: Schedule regular reviews of your payroll processes and records. This helps to catch any discrepancies early and ensures you consistently apply the latest tax rates and guidelines.
- Seek Professional Advice: When in doubt, consulting with a tax professional can provide clarity and guidance. This is especially helpful if you're navigating complex situations, such as multi-state operations or significant changes in your business structure or employee compensation packages.

Handling payroll taxes with care and diligence underscores the trust your employees place in you as an employer. It reflects your commitment to their well-being and the broader community through compliance with tax laws. By breaking down the process into clear, manageable steps and staying informed, you can easily navigate payroll taxes, ensuring your business thrives while contributing positively to the social fabric.

6.3 BENEFITS MANAGEMENT FOR SMALL BUSINESSES: HOW TO OFFER COMPETITIVE PACKAGES

A team of dedicated employees is at the heart of every thriving small business. Attracting and retaining such talent often hinges on more than just the salary; the benefits package can set a small business apart. Crafting a benefits package that resonates with current and prospective employees requires a thoughtful approach, balancing cost with desirability, and aligning offerings with the needs and values of your team.

Assessing What Benefits to Offer

Identifying the right mix of benefits for your team starts with understanding the landscape of available options and assessing their relevance to your business context. The potential benefits range from health insurance and retirement plans to more contemporary offerings like flexible working hours or remote work options. Here's how to navigate this assessment:

- Survey Your Team: Engage directly with your employees to understand their needs and preferences. This can be done through surveys or one-on-one conversations.
- Benchmark Against Competitors: Look at what similar businesses in your industry and region offer. Staying competitive is key to attracting top talent.
- Evaluate Your Budget: Each benefit comes with a cost. It's important to weigh each option's value to your employees against the required financial investment.

This process empowers you to construct a benefits package that is both appealing to your employees and sustainable for your business.

Navigating the Benefits Marketplace

With an understanding of the benefits your business wishes to offer, the next step is to explore the marketplace to find suitable providers and plans. Health insurance, the cornerstone of any benefits package, can be particularly complex. Here are pointers to help you through this exploration:

- Use Online Marketplaces: Platforms like the Small Business Health Options Program (SHOP) can simplify the search for health insurance by offering a variety of plans catered to small businesses.
- Consult with Brokers: Health insurance brokers can offer personalized guidance, helping you find plans that match your specific needs and budget.
- Consider Professional Employer Organizations (PEOs): PEOs can offer small businesses access to a wider range of benefits typically available to larger companies, including competitive health insurance plans, by pooling the employees of multiple small businesses.

This step is about finding the right partners to bring your chosen benefits to life in a way that fits your business's budget and values.

Setting Up Benefit Plans

With providers selected, setting up your benefits plans involves several administrative steps. This process varies significantly between different types of benefits but generally includes:

- Defining Eligibility Criteria: Determine which employees are eligible for which benefits. Factors to consider are employment status (full-time vs part-time) or length of service.

- Understanding Enrollment Periods: Most benefits, especially health insurance, have specific enrollment periods during which employees can sign up or change their plans.
- Managing Contributions: Decide on the structure of any contributions to the benefits, such as how much of a health insurance premium will be covered by the employer vs. the employee.

Clear documentation and organization are crucial during this phase to ensure a smooth rollout of the benefits package to your team.

Communicating Benefits to Employees

The true value of a benefits package is only realized when your employees fully understand and utilize the offerings. Clear and effective communication is crucial:

- Create Comprehensive Guides: Develop detailed guides that explain each benefit, how to enroll, and any associated costs to employees. These should be written in plain language to ensure accessibility.
- Hold Information Sessions: Organize meetings or workshops where employees can ask questions and learn more about their benefits directly from providers or knowledgeable team members.
- Provide Ongoing Support: Establish a point of contact within your business for benefits-related inquiries. Ensuring employees have somewhere to turn with

questions encourages engagement with the benefits package.

Thoughtful communication helps employees appreciate the value of their benefits and reinforces their understanding of your investment in their well-being.

Crafting a competitive benefits package is a dynamic process, reflecting the evolving needs of your employees and the changing landscape of benefit options. A well-designed package is a powerful tool for attracting and retaining talent and demonstrates your commitment to your team's health, happiness, and overall success. By carefully assessing the needs of your workforce, navigating the marketplace with diligence, setting up benefit plans with precision, and communicating with clarity, you can build a benefits package that truly stands out, contributing significantly to the culture and appeal of your small business.

6.4 DEALING WITH PAYROLL ISSUES: COMMON PROBLEMS AND HOW TO SOLVE THEM

Navigating payroll complexities can sometimes feel like steering through uncharted waters. Even with meticulous planning, issues such as payroll errors, late payments, and managing advances can arise, testing the resilience of your business operations. This section provides practical advice on addressing these hurdles, ensuring your payroll remains accurate, and your team stays content.

Correcting Payroll Errors

Payroll mistakes, be it overpayments, underpayments, or misclassifications, can disrupt the harmony within your team and potentially lead to legal complications. Here's how to address them effectively:

- Immediate Acknowledgment: As soon as an error is identified, acknowledge it to the affected employee(s). Transparency builds trust and can ease potential tensions.
- Swift Correction: For overpayments, discuss repayment options that don't impose undue hardship on the employee. For underpayments, compensate for the difference promptly.
- Review and Revise: Investigate the root cause of the error. Was it a data entry mistake or a misunderstanding of tax codes? Rectifying the underlying issue prevents recurrence.
- Document Everything: Keep detailed records of the error and how it was corrected. This documentation is crucial for both internal records and potential audits.

Addressing payroll errors quickly and sincerely remedies the immediate issue and strengthens your team's confidence in your management.

Handling Late Payroll

Delayed payroll can erode employee trust and lead to legal consequences, given the strict regulations surrounding timely wage payments. If you anticipate a delay, consider these steps:

- Pre-emptive Communication: Notify your team as soon as you foresee a delay. Explain the situation, the expected resolution time, and how you plan to prevent future occurrences.

- Explore Temporary Solutions: If the delay is due to a cash flow hiccup, look into short-term financing options like a business line of credit to meet your payroll obligations.
- Understand Legal Obligations: Familiarize yourself with the laws governing your jurisdiction's late-wage payments. Some areas may require additional compensation to employees for delays.

Keeping your team informed and seeking immediate remedies can help mitigate the impact of late payroll on employee morale and your business reputation.

Managing Employee Advances and Loans

Advances and loans can aid employees in times of need, but managing them requires careful consideration to avoid complications. Here's a guide to handling these requests prudently:

- Establish a Clear Policy: Define when advances or loans are allowed, the maximum amount, repayment terms, and interest charges. This policy ensures fairness and transparency.
- Document Agreements: For each advance or loan, document the agreed-upon terms, including repayment schedules. Both the employer and employee should sign this document.
- Payroll Deductions for Repayment: Set up a payroll deduction plan for repayment. Ensure that these deductions do not bring the employee's wages below the legal minimum wage.
- Tax Considerations: Consult with a tax professional regarding the tax implications of employee loans, especially if interest-free or at below-market interest rates.

A structured approach to advances and loans protects the business and the employee, providing a safety net while maintaining financial and legal integrity.

Updating Payroll for Changes in Employee Status

Changes in employee status, such as promotions, terminations, or tax status changes, necessitate updates to payroll. Failure to accurately reflect these changes can lead to errors and dissatisfaction. Here's how to manage updates effectively:

- Prompt Updates: Implement changes in payroll as soon as they occur. Delays can lead to incorrect payments and additional adjustments down the line.
- Communication with HR: Ensure a seamless flow of information between HR and your payroll department or provider. This coordination is critical for timely updates.
- Adjust Tax Withholdings: Changes in compensation or employee-initiated adjustments to withholdings require immediate attention to ensure accurate tax deductions.
- Final Paychecks: Be aware of the laws governing final paychecks for terminated employees. Some jurisdictions require that final pay be issued immediately, while others allow for the regular pay cycle.

Staying atop changes in employee status and adjusting payroll accordingly is key to maintaining an accurate payroll system. It reflects your respect for your team and commitment to upholding your responsibilities as an employer.

By adopting these strategies, you can confidently navigate common payroll challenges. Addressing issues promptly and transparently ensures compliance with legal standards and fosters a positive and trusting work environment. Your diligence in managing payroll intricacies speaks volumes about your commitment to your employees and the success of your business.

6.5 OUTSOURCING PAYROLL: PROS, CONS, AND HOW TO CHOOSE A PROVIDER

Deciding to outsource payroll is like making your bread in-house or sourcing it from the best bakery in town. Both options have their merits, but choosing the latter could mean saving valuable time and resources, though it comes with its own considerations.

Outsourcing payroll functions can significantly lighten your administrative load, allowing you to focus more on strategic aspects of your business. On the flip side, it requires entrusting a crucial part of your business operations to a third party, necessitating a careful selection process to ensure your provider is up to the task.

Weighing the Decision to Outsource

The decision to outsource payroll hinges on several factors, each worth careful consideration:

- Cost Benefits: Outsourcing can be a cost-effective solution for businesses without the in-house expertise to manage payroll effectively. It eliminates the need for dedicated payroll staff and the associated overhead expenses.
- Time Savings: By handing off payroll responsibilities, you reclaim hours that can be redirected towards growth-focused activities, enhancing your business's potential.
- Access to Expertise: Payroll providers bring specialized knowledge and stay abreast of changing regulations,

ensuring compliance and reducing the risk of errors or penalties.

- Flexibility and Scalability: As your business grows, a reputable payroll provider can scale their services to meet your evolving needs effortlessly.

However, weighing these benefits against potential drawbacks, such as the perceived loss of control over payroll processes and reliance on an external party for sensitive data handling, is essential.

Evaluating Payroll Providers

Selecting the right payroll provider is critical. Here are the criteria to guide your evaluation:

- Features: Look for providers offering comprehensive services, including tax filing, direct deposit, and detailed payroll reports. Integration with your existing HR systems is a plus.
- Customer Service: Opt for providers known for outstanding customer support, capable of addressing issues promptly and effectively.
- Cost: Compare pricing models to find a service that fits your budget. Be wary of hidden fees for additional services.
- Compliance Support: Ensure the provider has a strong track record of compliance. They should be able to manage tax filings accurately and on time, minimizing your exposure to penalties.

BOOKKEEPING MASTERY FOR SMALL BUSINESSES | 125

Implementing Outsourced Payroll

Transitioning to an outsourced payroll provider requires careful planning:

- Data Transfer: Organize and securely transfer employee data to the new provider, including personal information, tax details, and historical payroll data.
- Employee Communication: Keep your team informed about the change in payroll processing. Explain how and when they will receive their pay and whom to contact with questions.
- Training: If the provider offers a portal or tools for employee self-service, arrange training sessions to ensure everyone is comfortable using the new system.

A smooth transition sets the stage for a successful partnership and maintains trust and transparency with your employees.

Monitoring Outsourced Payroll Services

Even after you've outsourced payroll, staying engaged with the process is vital:

- Regular Reviews: Schedule periodic reviews of payroll reports and reconciliations to ensure accuracy. This also helps you stay informed about your business's financial status.
- Feedback Loop: Establish a clear channel for feedback with your provider. Regular communication can help identify issues early and foster continuous improvement.

- Stay Informed: Keep abreast of payroll and tax regulations. This knowledge allows you to evaluate the provider's performance against compliance standards.

Maintaining oversight ensures that the payroll service meets your business's needs and complies with regulatory requirements.

In wrapping up, outsourcing payroll comes with a blend of opportunities and considerations. By carefully evaluating potential providers, planning the transition meticulously, and maintaining oversight, you can enjoy the benefits of outsourcing while minimizing the drawbacks. This approach ensures that your employee's pay is accurate and timely and frees you to focus on the strategic initiatives that drive your business forward.

As we move forward, remember that every decision made in finance and operations, including payroll, is a step toward sculpting the future of your business. Your choices today lay the groundwork for the success and growth you'll enjoy tomorrow.

7

FINANCIAL STRATEGIES FOR GROWING YOUR BUSINESS

I magine you're at your favorite coffee shop, sipping on your go-to drink, watching the barista craft each beverage with precision. Running a business, much like brewing the perfect cup of coffee, demands a blend of the right ingredients, timing, and a bit of flair. This chapter will stir in financial strategies to help your business grow robust and flavorful.

7.1 BUDGETING FOR GROWTH: PLANNING YOUR FINANCIAL ROADMAP

Emphasizing the Importance of a Growth Budget

A growth budget isn't just about tracking expenses and revenue; it's your blueprint for future expansion. It aligns your financial goals with your business aspirations, ensuring you allocate resources to sustain and scale. Think of it as planning a road trip – you need a map, a destination, and enough gas to get you there. Your growth budget pinpoints where to invest, whether in marketing, product development, or new hires, to drive your business forward.

Incorporating Growth Projections into Budgeting

Accurate growth projections are the compass that guides your budgeting process. They help you anticipate revenue spikes, seasonal fluctuations, or market downturns. Here's how to get started:

- Review past performance: Analyze your business's historical data to identify growth patterns and trends.
- Market research: Stay informed about industry dynamics and how they might affect your business.
- Set realistic goals: Use this data to set achievable targets for sales, revenue, and other key metrics.

Mapping out your growth projections gives you a clearer picture of what resources you'll need at different stages, ensuring you're always one step ahead.

Adjusting the Budget for Scalability

A static budget is like a static business – it doesn't grow. Adaptability is key. Regularly revisiting and revising your budget ensures it evolves with your business. It's like adjusting your sails when the wind changes direction. Here are a few triggers that might prompt a budget review:

- New opportunities: A chance to enter a new market or launch a new product line.
- Unexpected challenges: Supply chain issues, changing regulations, or shifts in consumer behavior.

- Performance variances: Deviations from your growth projections, whether positive or negative.

Adjusting your budget for scalability means you're always prepared, regardless of the business climate.

Allocating Resources for Unexpected Opportunities

In business, as in life, opportunities can come knocking when least expected. Setting aside a portion of your budget for these opportunities ensures you can act swiftly without derailing your financial plans. It's the financial equivalent of keeping an extra seat at the table. This could mean:

- Investing in new technology that could streamline operations.
- Capitalizing on a sudden market demand for a product or service you offer.
- Exploring strategic partnerships that could open new avenues for growth.

Allocating resources for unexpected opportunities means you're ready for what you know is coming and the surprises that could propel your business forward.

Remember, crafting your growth budget is more than just numbers on a spreadsheet. It's a living document that reflects your business's aspirations, challenges, and the strategies you'll employ to overcome them. Like the barista at your favorite coffee shop, perfecting the art of coffee-making, your growth budget is about blending the right ingredients to create something remarkable. Whether investing in marketing to attract more customers, developing new products that set you apart, or expanding your team to increase capacity, your budget is the roadmap that will guide these decisions. But it's not set in stone. Regular reviews and adjustments ensure it remains aligned with your evolving business landscape, enabling you to seize new opportunities and navigate unexpected challenges. With a well-planned growth budget, you're not just running your business but steering it towards success.

7.2 FINANCING YOUR BUSINESS EXPANSION: OPTIONS AND CONSIDERATIONS

Securing the capital needed for your business's growth can often feel like navigating a dense forest with no clear path. Yet, understanding the landscape of financing options available can illuminate your way, guiding you toward the resources necessary for expansion.

Exploring Financing Options

Various funding avenues exist, each with its own set of advantages and prerequisites. Here's a closer look at some of the primary sources:

- Bank Loans: Traditional yet reliable bank loans offer a fixed amount of money with an interest rate and repayment schedule. Ideal for businesses with a solid credit history and financial statements.
- Investor Funding: This involves exchanging equity in your business for capital. Angel investors and venture capitalists are common sources suitable for businesses with high growth potential and a willingness to share control.
- Grants: Often overlooked, grants provide funds without needing repayment, though they come with specific conditions and are highly competitive. They're particularly

beneficial for businesses in particular industries or those contributing to social causes.

Each option serves different business needs and growth stages, making it crucial to align your choice with your expansion strategy.

Assessing the Cost of Financing

While securing funding is a win, it's vital to understand the actual cost tied to each option:

- Interest Rates: Loans come with interest rates, which can vary widely. Calculating the total interest over the loan period is essential to gauge its affordability.
- Repayment Terms: Terms can range from short-term (a few months) to long-term (several years). Longer terms might lower monthly payments but increase the total interest paid.
- Equity Dilution: Investor funding doesn't incur debt but does dilute ownership. Evaluate how much control you're willing to relinquish and the investor's role in decision-making.

Assessing these factors helps make an informed decision, ensuring the financing option strengthens rather than burdens your business growth.

Preparing for Lender or Investor Meetings

Meeting with potential lenders or investors is similar to a job interview for your business. Preparation is key. Here's how to make a compelling case:

- Financial Statements: Present up-to-date financial statements, including balance sheets, income statements, and cash flow statements. These documents offer a snapshot of your business's financial health.
- Business Plan: Your business plan should outline your growth strategy, market analysis, competitive landscape, and financial projections. It demonstrates your vision and how the requested funds will fuel growth.
- The Ask: Clearly articulate how much funding you seek, how it will be used, and the anticipated return on investment. Be ready to discuss your repayment plan or how investors will benefit.

Being well-prepared boosts your confidence and shows potential financiers that you're a smart investment.

Choosing the Right Financing Option

Selecting the best financing route for your business expansion is a critical decision that depends on several factors:

- Financial Health of Your Business: Assess your current financial situation. Businesses with strong sales and a solid credit history might find bank loans more accessible and cost-effective. Startups with high growth potential might be more attractive to investors.
- Growth Objectives: Align the financing option with your growth goals. If you're looking to expand quickly and are open to input and partnership, investor funding could be the way to go. For more controlled, steady growth, a loan might be better suited.
- Cost of Financing: Consider the total cost of financing and its impact on your business's cash flow. A loan with

favorable terms might be more beneficial in the long run than giving up a significant equity stake to investors.

In essence, the right financing option is one that not only provides the capital needed for growth but does so in a way that aligns with your business's values, objectives, and financial health. It's about finding a partner in growth, whether that's a financial institution, an investor, or a grant-making body, who believes in your vision and offers terms that propel, rather than restrict, your expansion journey.

By carefully navigating these considerations, you can illuminate the path forward, securing the funding needed to expand your business and reach new heights. Every business is unique, as is the journey to finance its growth. With the right strategy, preparation, and understanding of the options at hand, you can find the financial support that best suits your business's needs and aspirations, fueling your climb to new peaks of success.

7.3 MANAGING DEBT WISELY: STRATEGIES FOR SMALL BUSINESSES

Navigating the financial waters of debt management is like walking a tightrope. On one side, there's the growth potential, and on the other, the risk of falling into a pit of financial distress. This delicate balance is best maintained with a clear understanding of good versus bad debt, strategic planning, and vigilant monitoring.

Understanding Good Debt vs. Bad Debt

Debt often carries a negative connotation, yet not all debt is detrimental to your business. Distinguishing between debt that propels your business forward and debt that hinders progress is crucial.

- Good Debt is characterized by its potential to increase your business's value or generate income. This might include loans to purchase essential equipment, expand operations, or invest in marketing strategies that promise a high return on investment. The hallmark of good debt is its capacity to pay for itself over time.
- Bad Debt, on the other hand, does not contribute to your business's growth or has no potential return. Borrowing to cover recurring expenses or using high-interest credit cards for non-essential purchases could fall into this category. Bad debt often results from impulsive decisions or a lack of planning and can quickly escalate, stifling cash flow and growth.

Strategies for Debt Repayment

Effectively managing and repaying debt requires a tactical approach. Here are strategies designed to keep your business's debt load in check:

- Debt Consolidation: Combining multiple debts into a single loan, typically with a lower interest rate. It simplifies repayment and can reduce monthly outflows, freeing up cash for other uses.
- Refinancing: Similar to consolidation, refinancing focuses on obtaining a new loan with more favorable terms to pay off existing debt. Such as lower interest rates or extended repayment periods, which can ease the financial strain on your business.
- Negotiated Repayment Plans: Engaging creditors to negotiate repayment terms can result in more manageable payment schedules or reduced debt amounts. Creditors are

often willing to consider adjustments to ensure they recover a portion of the debt.

Implementing these strategies requires a thorough analysis of your current debt situation, including the terms, interest rates, and monthly payments of existing debts. This analysis will inform which strategy—or combination thereof—will be most effective for your business.

Monitoring Debt Levels

A proactive stance towards debt management includes regularly monitoring your business's debt levels. This vigilance ensures that debt remains a tool for growth rather than a barrier. Key aspects of monitoring include:

- Debt-to-Income Ratio: This metric helps gauge the health of your business's finances, indicating whether earnings are sufficient to cover debt obligations.
- Cash Flow Impact: Assessing how debt repayments affect your monthly cash flow is vital. Ensuring sufficient funds for debt servicing and operational expenses is crucial for maintaining stability.
- Interest Rate Fluctuations: For variable-rate loans, staying alert to interest rate changes can prevent unexpected increases in repayment amounts.

Regular reviews of your debt situation allow for timely adjustments to your repayment strategies, ensuring that debt levels remain sustainable.

Using Debt to Leverage Growth

Debt can be an effective tool for business expansion and innovation when managed wisely. Leveraging debt for growth involves:

- Strategic Borrowing: Only take on new debt for investments that promise a clear return, such as expanding into a new market or launching a product. The anticipated increase in revenue from these ventures should exceed the cost of the debt.
- Maintaining a Buffer: Always maintain a safety margin in your borrowing, ensuring you can still meet your debt obligations even if income projections fall short.
- Continuous Investment in Value-Adding Activities: Use debt to finance activities that add value to your business and enhance its competitive edge. Technology upgrades, staff training, or research and development are potential value-added activities.

The strategic use of debt for growth hinges on disciplined planning, a thorough assessment of potential returns, and a commitment to maintaining a balance between leveraging opportunities and managing risks.

In essence, managing debt within a small business context is not about avoidance but strategic engagement. It is understanding debt's nuanced role in your business's financial ecosystem and wielding it precisely to navigate challenges and seize growth opportunities. Whether it's through discerning the nature of the debt, employing innovative repayment strategies, diligently monitoring debt levels, or leveraging debt as a tool for expansion, the goal remains to ensure that debt serves as a stepping stone to greater financial health and business growth.

7.4 SCALING YOUR BOOKKEEPING PRACTICES: KEEPING UP WITH GROWTH

When a business starts to flourish, its bookkeeping needs evolve dramatically. The quaint ledger books or simple spreadsheets that once sufficed must be revised. As transaction volumes swell and financial operations become more intricate, your bookkeeping practices must mature in tandem. This evolution is not just about adding more columns to a spreadsheet; it's about rethinking how financial data is captured, processed, and analyzed to support informed decision-making as your business scales.

Adapting Bookkeeping for a Growing Business

Growth brings complexity to revenue streams, expense categories, and regulatory requirements. This complexity demands that your bookkeeping practices mature, ensuring they can handle increased transaction volume and diverse financial activities without compromising accuracy or timeliness. Adapting involves:

- Segmenting financial data to reflect different revenue streams or business units offers more precise insights into each segment's performance.
- Automating repetitive tasks such as invoicing and bill payments to reduce manual errors and free up time for strategic financial analysis.
- Enhancing financial controls to prevent fraud and ensure data integrity as more hands touch your financial processes.

This adaptation is akin to upgrading a car's engine to keep pace with the demands of a more challenging race track. The goal is to ensure your bookkeeping practices are robust enough to deliver the financial insights needed to drive your business forward.

Implementing Scalable Bookkeeping Solutions

Scalable solutions are the cornerstone of effective bookkeeping in a growing business. Cloud-based software shines in this arena, offering flexibility, accessibility, and integration capabilities that traditional bookkeeping methods cannot match. Key benefits include:

- Real-time data access allows up-to-the-minute financial insights from anywhere, at any time.
- Seamless integration with other business tools such as CRM systems, payroll services, and e-commerce platforms, ensuring all financial data is synchronized and up-to-date.
- Scalability to accommodate the expanding needs of your business without significant additional investment in new hardware or software.

Choosing the right cloud-based solution involves:

- Assessing your current and future bookkeeping needs.
- Evaluating the software's security features.
- Considering the ease of migration from your existing system.

It's a decision that lays the foundation for efficient and effective financial management as your business grows.

Outsourcing vs. In-House Bookkeeping

As your business expands, so does the decision to manage book-keeping in-house or outsource it to a specialist firm. Each option has its merits and considerations:

- In-house bookkeeping offers direct control over financial data and processes. It can benefit businesses with specific reporting needs or those operating in industries with stringent regulatory compliance requirements. However, as the business grows, so does the need for a larger, more specialized finance team, which can be a significant overhead cost.
- Outsourcing bookkeeping functions can be a cost-effective solution for businesses looking to leverage expertise without the expense of hiring a full-time finance team. It provides access to a team of specialists familiar with the latest accounting standards and technologies. The trade-off, however, is a potential decrease in control over your financial data and processes, making selecting a reputable and reliable outsourcing partner crucial.

Balancing the pros and cons involves considering factors like the complexity of your financial operations, the strategic importance of having an in-house finance team, and the cost implications of both options.

Ensuring Compliance at Scale

As businesses scale, they often cross new regulatory thresholds, whether due to entering new markets, hiring more employees, or increasing sales volumes. Each milestone can introduce new compliance requirements, making adherence to financial regulations an increasingly complex challenge. Key strategies to ensure compliance include:

- Regularly updating compliance knowledge to stay abreast of changes in tax laws, financial reporting standards, and industry-specific regulations. Subscribing to regulatory updates, attending seminars, or consulting with legal and financial advisors are good ways to stay informed.
- Automating compliance processes using software that can adapt to changing regulations, calculate taxes accurately, and generate reports that meet regulatory standards.
- Conduct regular financial audits to validate the accuracy of your financial records and ensure compliance with all applicable laws and regulations. These audits can be performed internally or by an external firm, depending on the size and complexity of your business.

Ensuring compliance is not just about avoiding penalties; it's about building trust with stakeholders, from investors to customers, by demonstrating your commitment to ethical and responsible financial management.

As your business grows, the need for sophisticated bookkeeping practices becomes increasingly apparent. Adapting these practices to match the pace of your expansion, selecting scalable solutions, making informed decisions on outsourcing versus in-house management, and ensuring compliance are all critical steps in supporting scalable growth. These strategies provide the financial insights needed to make informed decisions and ensure your business remains agile, responsive, and poised for continued success in an ever-changing business landscape.

7.5 INVESTING IN YOUR BUSINESS: FINANCIAL CONSIDERATIONS FOR LONG-TERM SUCCESS

When it's time to fuel growth within your venture, pinpointing where to channel your funds can transform potential into palpable success. This decision-making process is similar to a chef selecting the finest ingredients; it's about discerning quality and understanding the impact of each choice on the final dish.

Identifying Areas for Investment

The landscape of potential investment areas within a business is vast, yet certain zones consistently prove fertile for planting seeds of growth. These might include:

- Technology and Innovation: Keeping abreast of technological advancements can significantly enhance efficiency and open new revenue streams.
- Marketing and Brand Development: Strategic investments here can amplify your market presence and attract new customers.
- Employee Training and Development: Equipping your team with new skills fosters innovation and improves service delivery.
- Product or Service Expansion: Broadening your offerings can meet untapped customer needs or enter new markets.

Deciphering where investments will have the most substantial impact requires a deep dive into your business analytics. Look for areas with the highest return potential, and consider where investments could safeguard against emerging threats or industry shifts.

Evaluating Investment ROI

The return on investment (ROI) metric is pivotal in evaluating the effectiveness of each potential investment. Calculating ROI involves comparing the gain from an investment against its cost. However, it's crucial to consider both tangible and intangible returns. For instance, investing in employee training might not yield immediate financial returns but can significantly improve operational efficiency and employee satisfaction over time.

When evaluating ROI:

- Factor in both direct and indirect returns. Increased sales are a direct return, while enhanced brand loyalty is an indirect return.
- Allow for a realistic time frame. Some investments, especially in branding or R&D, might take longer to mature.

This analysis ensures that each dollar invested works towards your business's strategic goals, yielding immediate and long-term benefits.

Balancing Short-Term Costs with Long-Term Gains

Investing in growth often requires upfront expenditures that might strain your current financial resources. It's like planting a garden; the initial labor and cost of seeds precede the harvest. Balancing these short-term costs with the anticipated long-term gains is crucial. Strategies to maintain this balance include:

- Prioritizing investments with quicker paybacks to sustain cash flow.

- Phasing larger projects to spread out costs.
- Monitoring cash reserves to ensure operational stability.

Maintaining this equilibrium ensures that your business remains financially healthy while pursuing growth.

Funding Business Investments

Once you've identified and evaluated key areas for investment, securing the necessary capital is the next step. Beyond traditional financing and investor funding, there are creative avenues to explore:

- Reinvesting Profits: Returning earnings to your business is a powerful way to fund growth without incurring debt.
- Crowdfunding: This can validate your product in the market while raising funds.
- Strategic Partnerships: Collaborating with other businesses can provide access to resources and split costs.

Each funding source has implications for your business's financial health and autonomy. Thus, selecting the right mix is vital to support your growth objectives without compromising your business's foundation.

In navigating the investment landscape, the key lies in making informed, strategic decisions that align with your long-term vision for your business. It's about seeing beyond the immediate horizon, anticipating how today's investments will shape tomorrow's success. From identifying ripe areas for investment and assessing their potential return, balancing the scales between current expenditures and future gains, and choosing the right funding avenues, each step is a building block toward achieving sustainable growth.

As we wrap up this exploration into strategic financial planning and investment, we're reminded of the broader narrative that business success is not just about surviving but thriving. It's about making calculated moves today that will ensure your business not only stands the test of time but also flourishes, carving out a legacy that lasts. With a keen eye on the future and a strategic investment approach, you're setting the stage for enduring success.

As we pivot towards our next discussion, remember that the business growth journey is a mosaic of strategic decisions, each influenced by thoughtful financial planning and a clear vision for the future.

8

BEYOND THE BASICS: ADVANCED BOOKKEEPING TECHNIQUES

P icture this: You've just wrapped up an exceptionally busy month, and it's time to tackle the bookkeeping. Instead of dreading the mountain of receipts, invoices, and bank statements, imagine if you could handle all this with a few clicks. Technology in bookkeeping isn't just about making tasks quicker; it's about transforming data into a strategic asset that propels your business forward. In this chapter, we explore how advanced software features, seamless system integration, and the power of data analytics can revolutionize how small businesses manage their finances.

8.1 LEVERAGING TECHNOLOGY: ADVANCED BOOKKEEPING SOFTWARE FEATURES

Exploring Advanced Software Features

The right bookkeeping software does more than track income and expenses; it becomes the financial hub of your business. Here's what to look for:

- Automation: Imagine software that categorizes expenses as soon as they occur, sends invoices automatically, and even follows up on unpaid ones. The time saved here can be redirected to growth-focused activities.
- Cloud-based Access: With cloud-based software, your financial data is at your fingertips, whether in the office or halfway across the world. This flexibility is invaluable for decision-making on the fly.
- Security: Advanced encryption and security protocols protect your financial data from unauthorized access, giving you peace of mind in an age where cyber threats are all too common.

When selecting software, consider the tasks that consume most of your time and see which platforms can take those off your plate.

Integrating Bookkeeping with Other Business Systems

Efficiency in bookkeeping comes from how well it plays with other systems you use. Integration is key. Here's why:

- Payroll Integration: Connect your bookkeeping software with your payroll system to streamline salary payments and financial reporting. This ensures accuracy across the board, from tax deductions to expense categorization.

- E-commerce Platforms: For businesses that sell online, linking your e-commerce platform with your bookkeeping software can automate sales reporting and inventory management, keeping your books up to date in real time.
- Customer Relationship Management (CRM): Integrating your CRM system can provide insights into customer behavior, payment history, and overall profitability, driving more informed business decisions.

This interconnected ecosystem saves time and provides a holistic view of your business operations, making it easier to identify opportunities and challenges.

Data Analytics and Reporting

In bookkeeping, data analytics is akin to turning raw ingredients into a gourmet meal. It's about extracting valuable insights from your financial data. Here's how:

- Trend Analysis: Spotting trends in your income and expenses can help predict future cash flow needs or identify areas where cost savings are possible.
- Performance Metrics: Software can track key performance indicators (KPIs) like profit margins, expense ratios, and more, benchmarking them against industry standards.
- Custom Reports: Tailor reports to your specific needs, whether tracking the profitability of a new product line or understanding the costs associated with a particular project.

With this information, you can make strategic decisions that drive growth and improve efficiency.

Choosing Software that Scales with Your Business

Your business isn't static, and your bookkeeping software shouldn't be either. Scalability is crucial. Here's what to consider:

- User Limits: Check if the software can accommodate increasing users as your team grows.
- Feature Expansion: Look for platforms that offer additional features or modules that can be added as your business needs evolve.
- Support and Training: Ensure the provider offers comprehensive support and training resources to help you maximize the software's potential.

Remember, investing in the right bookkeeping software is an investment in your business's future. It's about finding a solution that meets your current needs and can grow with you.

In wrapping up, transitioning to advanced bookkeeping software is more than a mere upgrade; it's a strategic move that can unlock new insights, drive efficiencies, and support your business's growth trajectory. By focusing on automation, integration, analytics, and scalability, you can transform your bookkeeping from a mandatory task to a powerful tool in your business arsenal.

8.2 ANALYZING FINANCIAL REPORTS: BEYOND THE BASICS

Venturing into advanced financial analysis opens doors to a deeper understanding of your business's performance, revealing insights that basic evaluations might miss. This section guides you through sophisticated techniques, benchmarking practices, forecasting methods, and risk management strategies to elevate your financial oversight.

Advanced Financial Analysis Techniques

Moving beyond basic profit and loss statements, advanced financial analysis delves into ratios, trends, and comparative assessments that offer a more precise view of your business's health. Techniques such as:

- Liquidity Ratios: Assess your company's ability to meet short-term obligations without raising external capital. Ratios like the current ratio and quick ratio offer insights into financial stability.
- Profitability Ratios: Gauge your business's ability to generate earnings relative to sales, assets, and equity. Metrics such as gross profit margin, return on assets (ROA) and return on equity (ROE) highlight efficiency and potential areas for improvement.
- Leverage Ratios: Examine the level of debt compared to equity within your business. Debt-to-equity and interest coverage ratios can indicate the risk level associated with your company's financial structure.

These techniques allow for a more dynamic analysis, providing a comprehensive picture of your business's financial standing.

Benchmarking Against Industry Standards

Comparing your financial metrics against industry benchmarks can offer valuable context, helping pinpoint where your business stands relative to peers. This process involves:

- Identifying relevant benchmarks that reflect industry averages for profitability, liquidity, and efficiency.
- This data can be sourced from industry reports, trade associations, or financial databases.
- Analyzing discrepancies between your metrics and these benchmarks to identify areas of strength and those requiring attention.

This comparison highlights competitive advantages and uncovers potential weaknesses, guiding strategic decisions to enhance performance.

Forecasting Future Financial Performance

Leveraging historical financial data for forecasting involves analyzing past trends to predict future financial outcomes. Effective forecasting can inform:

- Revenue projections, based on historical sales growth, adjusted for market conditions and business initiatives.
- Expense forecasts consider fixed and variable cost trends alongside planned investments.
- Cash flow predictions are crucial for ensuring liquidity and planning for capital expenditures or debt repayment.

BOOKKEEPING MASTERY FOR SMALL BUSINESSES | 151

Accurate forecasts enable proactive management, allowing for strategic adjustments in anticipation of future financial landscapes.

Identifying and Mitigating Financial Risks

Navigating financial risks requires a keen eye for potential pitfalls and implementing strategies to mitigate these threats. Key steps include:

- Regularly review financial statements and metrics for early signs of declining cash flow, increasing debt levels, or shrinking profit margins.
- Conducting scenario analysis to understand the financial impact of various risks, such as market downturns, supply chain disruptions, or changes in consumer behavior.
- Establishing financial safeguards, such as maintaining liquidity reserves, diversifying revenue streams, and securing fixed-rate financing to protect against interest rate hikes.

By actively identifying and addressing financial risks, you can safeguard your business's stability and ensure sustained growth.

This exploration into advanced financial analysis enriches your understanding of your business's financial health and empowers you to make informed decisions. From dissecting financial ratios to benchmarking against industry standards, forecasting future performance, and strategizing risk mitigation, each step strengthens your financial insight. With these tools at your disposal, navigating the financial aspects of your business becomes a more precise and strategic endeavor, setting a solid foundation for future success.

8.3 STRATEGIC TAX PLANNING: ADVANCED STRATEGIES FOR SMALL BUSINESSES

Navigating the labyrinth of tax regulations requires vigilance and a proactive strategy to ensure your business remains compliant and thrives. This segment delves into the nuanced world of strategic tax planning. It highlights the avenues small businesses can explore to optimize their tax obligations, adapt to legislative changes, harness tax deferral opportunities, and the invaluable asset of professional tax advice.

The taxation landscape is as dynamic as it is intricate, with continual adjustments and amendments to laws that can significantly impact your business's financial health. It's crucial, therefore, to not just react to these changes but to anticipate and prepare for them, ensuring your business leverages every tax benefit available while steering clear of potential pitfalls.

Tax Optimization Strategies

Tax optimization is akin to a finely tuned orchestra, where every element works harmoniously to create a symphony of savings and efficiencies. Here are key strategies:

- Maximizing Deductions and Credits: Start by ensuring you're claiming all the deductions and credits for which your business is eligible. This might include equipment purchases, research and development costs, and certain business travel expenses. Credits for hiring practices, environmental improvements, or research activities can also offer substantial savings.
- Income Splitting: If your business structure permits, consider income splitting to distribute income among

family members in lower tax brackets, reducing the overall tax burden.

- Capital Gains vs. Ordinary Income: Aim to structure your income to take advantage of lower tax rates on long-term capital gains compared to rates on ordinary income.

Planning for Tax Changes

Staying ahead of tax law changes is not just about compliance; it's a strategic advantage. This proactive stance involves:

- Regular Updates: Keep abreast of legislative developments at both federal and state levels. Tax laws can shift with political climates, and what was advantageous one year might be detrimental the next.
- Scenario Planning: Develop financial models based on potential tax changes. How would an increase in the corporate tax rate affect your bottom line? What if tax credits you rely on were decreased or eliminated?
- Flexibility in Financial Planning: Build flexibility into your financial strategy to adapt to new tax laws quickly. Deferring certain income into the next tax year or accelerating expenses to take advantage of current deductions could be helpful strategies.

Utilizing Tax Deferral Opportunities

Deferring tax obligations can significantly enhance your business's cash flow, freeing up capital for reinvestment in growth initiatives. Strategies include:

- Retirement Plans: Setting up retirement plans such as a 401(k) or SEP IRA not only benefits you and your employees but also allows for the deferral of taxes on contributions until withdrawal.

- Depreciation Strategies: Leveraging depreciation methods can defer taxes on capital purchases. For instance, the Modified Accelerated Cost Recovery System (MACRS) can accelerate depreciation deductions, defer taxes, and improve near-term cash flow.
- Inventory Management: For certain businesses, choosing between different inventory valuation methods (e.g., FIFO vs. LIFO) can impact the timing of tax liabilities, offering deferral opportunities.

Seeking Professional Tax Advice

The complexities of tax planning underscore the value of professional advice. A seasoned tax professional can offer the following:

- Customized Strategies: Tailored advice based on your specific business structure, industry, and financial goals. This bespoke approach ensures that tax planning fully integrates with your business strategy.
- Audit Support: In the event of an audit, having a tax professional who is familiar with your business can be invaluable. They can guide the process, ensuring your rights are protected, and the audit is conducted fairly.
- Ongoing Partnership: Consider your tax advisor a year-round partner, not just someone you consult during tax season. Regular meetings help identify new tax-saving opportunities and ensure your business adjusts to changing tax laws and financial conditions.

Strategic tax planning is an ongoing process that requires attention, adaptability, and expertise. By maximizing deductions and credits, staying informed and prepared for tax law changes, leveraging tax deferral opportunities, and seeking professional advice, small businesses can not only navigate the complexities of taxation but turn them into a strategic advantage. This proactive approach ensures compliance and optimizes your tax position, enhancing your business's financial health and supporting its growth objectives.

8.4 CUSTOMIZING YOUR BOOKKEEPING SYSTEM: TAILORING FOR INDUSTRY-SPECIFIC NEEDS

In the tapestry of modern commerce, each industry weaves its unique pattern, with distinct threads representing its financial transactions, regulatory landscapes, and operational challenges. Recognizing and adapting your bookkeeping system to these unique characteristics enhances compliance and efficiency and sharpens your competitive edge. This approach enables businesses to capture relevant financial insights, driving strategic decisions that foster growth and sustainability.

Industry-Specific Bookkeeping Considerations

Different arenas of business—from the bustling world of retail to the precision-driven realm of manufacturing—each bring their financial management nuances. Retail operations, for instance, must meticulously track inventory turnover and manage vendor relationships, while construction firms navigate project-based accounting, incorporating costs across varying timelines and budgets. Service-oriented sectors like consulting prioritize time tracking and billable hours.

Understanding these distinctions is crucial. It informs the customization of your bookkeeping practices to meet daily operational needs and anticipate industry-specific financial challenges. Tailoring your system starts with a deep dive into your industry's financial pulse, identifying the metrics that truly matter—be it gross margin per project, average inventory period, or client acquisition cost.

Custom Reports and Dashboards

Armed with clarity on what drives financial success in your industry, the next step involves translating this into actionable insights through custom reports and dashboards. This process transforms raw data into strategic intelligence, illuminating paths to efficiency and growth. For a restaurant owner, a dashboard might highlight daily sales against food cost percentages, offering immediate visibility into profitability. A tech startup, on the other hand, might focus on burn rate and monthly recurring revenue, critical metrics for sustaining operations and attracting investors.

Creating these bespoke tools often starts within your bookkeeping software, leveraging its reporting functionalities to construct clear, insightful views of your financial health. This might involve:

- Setting up automated reports that track key performance indicators, delivered straight to your inbox or accessible via a mobile dashboard.
- Utilizing visualization tools within the software to create graphs and charts that make trends and patterns easily digestible at a glance.
- Customizing the layout and information density of reports and dashboards to match user preferences ensures that vital data is front and center.

Adapting to Regulatory Requirements

Each industry faces a labyrinth of regulations, from healthcare's stringent patient privacy laws to the environmental protections governing energy sectors. These regulations extend into financial management and reporting, dictating how transactions are recorded, how data is stored, and what information must be disclosed publicly.

Adapting your bookkeeping practices to these requirements is not merely about avoiding penalties; it's an exercise in fortifying trust with stakeholders and securing your business's reputation. This adaptation process may involve:

- Implementing data security measures that meet or exceed industry standards, ensuring that financial information remains confidential and secure.
- Developing documentation practices that create a clear, auditable trail of financial transactions, ready for regulatory review at a moment's notice.
- Staying agile and prepared to adjust bookkeeping practices in response to regulatory changes often requires keeping a finger on the pulse of legislative developments.

Implementing Best Practices

While each industry's financial landscape is unique, certain best practices are universal beacons, guiding businesses toward operational excellence and financial clarity. Implementing these practices within the context of your industry-specific needs can dramatically enhance the efficiency of your bookkeeping system. Considerations include:

- Regular reconciliation processes ensure your bookkeeping records mirror bank statements and inventory counts, which are critical steps for maintaining accuracy across all sectors.
- A commitment to continuous education, ensuring that your bookkeeping team (whether in-house or outsourced) remains informed about the latest industry trends, software updates, and regulatory changes.
- The integration of forward-looking financial planning and analysis, moving beyond mere record-keeping to strategic financial management that anticipates future industry shifts.

Incorporating these cornerstones of effective bookkeeping into a system tailored to your industry's specific rhythms streamlines daily operations and paves the way for informed, strategic decision-making. It ensures that your financial management practices are not just a reflection of past transactions but a lens focused on future opportunities and challenges.

In the journey of business growth and adaptation, recognizing the distinct financial blueprint of your industry is pivotal. It's about more than compliance and efficiency; it's about crafting a financial narrative that resonates with the unique rhythms of your sector, driving strategic decisions that propel your business forward. Customizing your bookkeeping system to align with industry-specific needs, leveraging custom reports and dashboards for deeper insights, adapting to regulatory landscapes, and implementing universal best practices—these steps create a robust framework for financial management that not only navigates the present complexities but also poised to embrace future opportunities.

8.5 FUTURE-PROOFING YOUR BOOKKEEPING: STAYING AHEAD OF REGULATORY CHANGES

In the dynamic world of business, one constant remains: change. Especially when it comes to the regulations that govern how we manage our finances and report our operations. Staying ahead of these shifts isn't just about keeping your business compliant; it's about turning adaptability into an advantage. Here, you'll discover methods for preempting changes in the regulatory landscape, the value of flexible bookkeeping systems, and the importance of a culture of continuous learning within your financial practices. Additionally, we will touch on the power of professional networks in keeping your finger on the pulse of best practices and regulatory updates.

Navigating through regulatory shifts requires a proactive stance. Here are strategies that can play a crucial role in ensuring you're not caught off guard:

- Regular Monitoring of Legislative Developments: Keeping up with changes in financial regulations is crucial. This can involve subscribing to updates from regulatory bodies, attending relevant industry seminars, and participating in forums where such changes are discussed.
- Scenario Planning: Consider how potential regulatory changes could impact your operations. Develop plans for various scenarios, which can help you respond quickly and effectively when changes occur.

Implementing bookkeeping systems that can swiftly adapt to new regulations ensures that your business remains compliant and efficient, regardless of how the regulatory landscape evolves. Key considerations include:

- Choosing Adaptable Software: Opt for bookkeeping software that offers regular updates in response to regulatory changes to ensure your system always remains compliant.
- Customization Capabilities: Systems that allow for customization can be quickly adjusted to accommodate new reporting requirements or financial practices as they arise.

Building a culture of continuous learning and adaptation within your bookkeeping practices prepares your team for regulatory changes and enhances overall efficiency. Ways to foster this culture include:

- Ongoing Training: Regular training sessions for your finance team on the latest bookkeeping practices and software functionalities ensure skills remain sharp and practices up to date.
- Encouraging Curiosity and Research: Promote an environment where team members are encouraged to stay informed about industry trends and share their findings.

Professional networks and resources are invaluable for staying ahead in the regulatory game. They offer insights, advice, and a heads-up on impending changes. Leveraging these networks involves:

- Joining Industry Associations: These organizations often provide members with updates on regulatory changes, best practices, and access to training resources.
- Engaging with Financial Advisors: Regular consultations with financial advisors can help you anticipate the impact of potential regulatory changes and strategize accordingly.

The landscape of business regulations is ever-evolving, influenced by economic shifts, technological advancements, and societal expectations. Staying ahead of these changes doesn't just prevent compliance headaches; it can also uncover opportunities for efficiency gains and strategic advantages. By anticipating regulatory changes, implementing flexible bookkeeping systems, fostering a culture of continuous learning, and leveraging professional networks, you can ensure that your bookkeeping practices are not just prepared for the future but are actively shaping it.

As we wrap up this exploration into the future-proofing of bookkeeping practices, it's clear that adaptability, foresight, and a proactive approach are essential. These strategies safeguard against the uncertainties of regulatory shifts and position your business to navigate these changes confidently. Moving forward, the focus will shift to exploring the integration of cutting-edge technologies and innovative methodologies in bookkeeping. This next step will delve into how these advancements can further refine, enhance, and revolutionize how we manage our finances, paving the way for even greater efficiency and strategic insight.

9

TURNING FINANCIAL CHALLENGES INTO OPPORTUNITIES

Have you ever noticed how a small leak can sink a great ship? Similarly, minor cash flow problems can capsize even the most robust small business if left unchecked. The good news is that these financial leaks can be plugged with the right know-how. This section is all about rolling up our sleeves and getting down to the nitty-gritty of solving cash flow problems, equipped with real-world solutions that have proven effective.

9.1 SOLVING CASH FLOW PROBLEMS: REAL-WORLD SOLUTIONS FOR SMALL BUSINESSES

Identifying Root Causes

First things first, let's shine a light on what's causing the cash flow crunch. Is it slow-paying customers, or perhaps overheads are sky-high? Sometimes, the problem could stem from not having a clear picture of incoming and outgoing cash. Identifying these root causes is like diagnosing a patient; it's crucial before any treatment plan.

- Late Payments: If customers take their sweet time to pay, it's time to reassess your invoicing strategy. Are your payment terms clear? Is it easy for customers to pay you?
- High Overheads: Look at your expenses. Sometimes, cutting back on non-essential spending or renegotiating supplier contracts can free up a lot of cash.
- Poor Cash Flow Management: Not having a clear view of your cash flow is like navigating a ship in foggy weather. Regular cash flow forecasts can help clear the mist.

Immediate Solutions

With the problem areas pinpointed, let's talk about quick fixes. These are like the first aid kit for your business's cash flow woes.

- Invoice Financing: This can be a lifesaver if late payments are a chronic issue. Services that offer invoice financing can advance you the money for outstanding invoices minus a fee. It's quick cash when you need it.
- Short-term Loans: Sometimes, you just need a stopgap to keep things running smoothly until better cash flow days. Short-term loans or lines of credit can be that buffer. Just be mindful of the interest rates and repayment terms.

Long-Term Strategies

Once the immediate fires are out, it's time to build a more resilient cash flow system. Think of this as the renovation phase after patching up leaks.

- Improving Invoicing Processes: Automated invoicing software can send reminders to customers and even thank them when payment is made. Also, consider offering multiple payment methods to make it easy for clients to pay you.
- Expense Management: Regularly review your expenses. Do you really need that fancy office space, or could you switch to a co-working space? Every little saving adds up.
- Building a Cash Reserve: Start setting aside a small percentage of income to create a cash reserve. It's your financial cushion for rainy days.

Case Studies

Now, let's look at some real-life scenarios where small businesses turned their cash flow around:

1. The Boutique That Got Creative with Inventory: A clothing boutique struggled with cash tied up in unsold inventory. They launched a series of pop-up sales and used social media marketing to drive traffic. The result? Increased sales and improved cash flow.
2. The Cafe That Brewed Up Prepaid Coffee Cards: Facing a downturn in foot traffic, a cafe introduced prepaid coffee cards. Customers could buy ten coffees in advance at a discount. This initiative boosted cash flow and customer loyalty.
3. The Freelancer Who Streamlined Payments: A freelance graphic designer was often left waiting for client payments. By switching to a cloud-based invoicing system with automated reminders and direct payment options, they drastically reduced payment times and improved cash flow.

Each of these businesses faced cash flow challenges but managed to navigate through them with strategic tweaks to their operations. It's a testament to the power of creativity, technology, and sometimes, just plain old good management practices in solving cash flow problems.

Remember, cash flow issues don't have to be the iceberg that sinks your business. With the right strategies, you can navigate financial challenges and steer your business toward calm, prosperous waters. Keep a keen eye on the root causes of cash flow problems, arm yourself with immediate solutions when times get tough, and always plan for the future with long-term strategies that ensure your business remains financially healthy and resilient.

9.2 TURNING FINANCIAL OBSTACLES INTO OPPORTUNITIES: A MINDSET SHIFT

When you hit a financial snag, it's easy to see it as a setback. But what if you viewed it as a hidden gem of opportunity instead? It's all about shifting your mindset. Seeing financial obstacles not as roadblocks but as chances to learn, grow, and innovate can transform your approach to business challenges.

Adopting a Growth Mindset

Imagine facing a sudden drop in sales. Instead of panicking, ask yourself what this challenge teaches you. Is it time to diversify your product line or explore new markets? This growth mindset turns a potentially paralyzing situation into a springboard for expansion. It's about asking the right questions: "What can we learn?" rather than "Why did this happen to us?"

Innovative Problem-Solving

Every financial obstacle carries the seeds of innovation. For example, a tight budget might inspire you to explore cost-effective marketing strategies, like leveraging social media or community-based events, which could open up new avenues for customer engagement. Here's how you could approach it:

- Brainstorming sessions: Regular team meetings focusing on creative problem-solving can unearth surprisingly effective solutions.
- Customer feedback: Directly engaging with your customers can provide insights into what they truly value, leading to cost-efficient ways to enhance your product or service offering.

Remember, some of the most successful products or services were born out of constraints. They say necessity is the mother of invention for a good reason.

Leveraging Challenges for Improvement

Every financial challenge you overcome strengthens your business's resilience and fine-tunes your operations. An example could be implementing more rigorous financial tracking mechanisms in response to cash flow issues. Resolving the immediate problem and enhancing your overall financial management, making your business leaner and more efficient. Key areas often ripe for improvement include:

- Operational efficiencies: Streamlining processes to reduce waste and increase productivity.

- Supplier negotiations: Working with suppliers to secure better terms or discounts.
- Customer payment policies: Introducing incentives for early payment or penalties for late payment to improve cash flow.

Success Stories

Let's look at a couple of businesses that flipped the script on financial obstacles, turning them into success stories:

- A local bakery found itself struggling with the high costs of ingredients. The owner decided to source locally, reducing costs and used this as a marketing point to attract customers interested in supporting local businesses. Sales soared, and the bakery secured a loyal customer base.
- A tech startup faced significant cash flow problems in its early stages. Instead of cutting back on product development, which would compromise its future, the company opted for equity crowdfunding. This provided the necessary funds and created a community of supporters who invested in the startup's success. The product launched to critical acclaim, and the startup secured additional funding based on its initial success.

These stories illustrate how viewing financial obstacles through a lens of opportunity can lead to innovative solutions that propel a business forward. The bakery's focus on local sourcing turned a cost-cutting measure into a unique selling point, while the tech startup's crowdfunding approach solved its cash flow problem and built a strong foundation of support.

Navigating the financial ups and downs of running a business, adopting a growth mindset, embracing innovative problem-solving, leveraging challenges for operational improvement, and drawing inspiration from success stories can transform potential setbacks into powerful opportunities for growth. This approach not only helps in overcoming immediate financial hurdles but also in building a more resilient, agile, and successful business.

9.3 LEARNING FROM FINANCIAL MISTAKES: HOW TO BOUNCE BACK STRONGER

Mistakes, especially financial ones, can feel like stumbling blocks. However, they also provide fertile ground for growth and learning. The trick lies in approaching these missteps not with dread but with curiosity and a commitment to improvement. This section aims to illuminate how small business owners can transform financial errors into stepping stones toward success.

Analyzing Mistakes for Learning

Every financial mistake carries with it a lesson waiting to be uncovered. The process begins with a thorough analysis, peeling back the layers to understand what went wrong and why. Here's a step-by-step approach to dissecting mistakes effectively:

- Gather all the facts: Compile all related documents, data, and correspondence. This comprehensive view is critical for an unbiased analysis.
- Map out the timeline: Trace the sequence of events leading to the mistake, often revealing where things started to veer off course.
- Identify decision points: Look for moments where different choices could have led to different outcomes.

These are valuable insights into how similar situations can be handled better in the future.

- Seek multiple perspectives: Involve team members who were part of the process. Their insights can provide a fuller understanding and might highlight aspects you overlooked.

Implementing Corrective Measures

Once the lessons are learned, the next step is implementing measures to prevent recurrence. This isn't about quick fixes but systemic changes that fortify your business against similar missteps. Consider the following strategies:

- Update policies and procedures: If a mistake stemmed from a lack of clear guidelines, revising existing policies or creating new ones can provide clarity and direction.
- Invest in training: Sometimes, mistakes happen due to gaps in knowledge or skills. Targeted training sessions can bridge these gaps, enhancing your team's competence.
- Leverage technology: Many financial errors arise from manual processes that are prone to human error. Automating these processes with software can reduce these risks significantly.
- Regular reviews: Implement a system of regular financial audits or reviews. This proactive approach can catch potential issues before they escalate into problems.

Building a Culture of Transparency

A culture that shies away from discussing mistakes is doomed to repeat them. Creating an environment where financial errors are openly discussed without fear of blame or retribution is key to learning and growth. Here's how to foster such a culture:

- Lead by example: Share your experiences with financial mistakes and the lessons learned. This sets a tone of openness and humility.
- Encourage sharing: Regular meetings where team members share challenges, mistakes, and lessons learned can be incredibly valuable. It's about creating a safe space for constructive conversations.
- Reframe the narrative: Instead of focusing on the mistake itself, focus on the learning and corrective measures. This positive framing can change how your team perceives and reacts to financial missteps.
- Celebrate resilience: Acknowledge and celebrate the ability to bounce back from mistakes. Reinforcing the value of resilience and encouraging a constructive response to challenges.

Resilience and Recovery

The path to financial recovery post-mistake is as much about mindset as it is about action. Resilience, the ability to recover from setbacks, is a muscle that strengthens with use. Below are strategies to build this resilience:

- Set realistic goals: Break down the recovery process into manageable steps. Achieving these smaller goals can boost confidence and provide momentum.
- Focus on what you can control: It's easy to get overwhelmed by the aspects of the situation that are beyond your control. Concentrate your efforts on areas where you can make a difference.

- Maintain perspective: Remember, most financial mistakes are not fatal. Keeping the bigger picture in mind helps to maintain balance and avoid getting bogged down by setbacks.
- Seek support: Whether from mentors, peers, or financial advisors, don't hesitate to ask for advice and support. Sometimes, an external perspective can offer clarity and solutions you might not have considered.

Every financial mistake holds within it the seeds of growth and improvement. The key lies in approaching these errors with a mindset geared towards learning and resilience. By carefully analyzing where things went awry, implementing measures to prevent future occurrences, fostering a culture that views mistakes as learning opportunities, and focusing on recovery and resilience, small business owners can navigate the tumultuous waters of financial management with greater confidence and capability. This approach helps mitigate the impact of current mistakes and lays a strong foundation for a more robust and resilient financial future.

9.4 BUILDING A FINANCIAL SUPPORT NETWORK: FINDING TRUSTED ADVISORS AND RESOURCES

In small business finance, having a robust support network isn't just beneficial; it's a lifeline that can keep you afloat in turbulent waters. This network, comprising seasoned professionals and peers, offers guidance, wisdom, and, sometimes, the much-needed reality check to navigate complex financial landscapes. Here's how to cultivate this invaluable resource.

Identifying Key Advisors

Key advisors are at the core of your financial support network - individuals whose expertise can significantly impact your financial strategy and execution. Finding the right mix of advisors involves more than just Googling 'best financial advisor near me.' Here's a structured approach:

- Accountants and Financial Planners: These professionals should have stellar qualifications and experience in your specific industry. They can offer tailored advice on tax planning, financial forecasting, and investment strategies.
- Mentors: Look for mentors who have successfully navigated the journey you're on. Drawing from real-world experiences, their insights can be gold dust in avoiding pitfalls and seizing opportunities.
- Legal Advisors: Given the myriad of laws governing small businesses, having a legal advisor familiar with your industry can save you from legal headaches down the line.

Start by listing what you need help with, then seek professionals who fill those gaps. Remember, the goal is to build a team that complements your skills and knowledge.

Utilizing Online Resources

The digital age has systematized access to financial advice and support. Numerous online platforms now offer resources that industry insiders once gatekept. Here's how to leverage these resources:

- Financial Blogs and Websites: Sites like Investopedia or the Small Business Administration offer a wealth of information on financial management, planning, and strategies tailored to small businesses.

- Webinars and Online Courses: Many financial institutions and consulting firms host webinars that can deepen your understanding of complex financial concepts and current market trends.
- Forums and Online Communities: Platforms like Reddit's r/smallbusiness or industry-specific forums are treasure troves of advice, experiences, and strategies shared by fellow business owners.

While navigating these resources, critically evaluate the information and consider how it applies to your unique business context. Not all advice is one-size-fits-all.

Joining Industry Associations

Industry associations can be gateways to specialized knowledge, resources, and networking opportunities. Membership often comes with perks like access to industry reports, financial management tools, and invitations to conferences and workshops. Here's what you stand to gain:

- Networking Opportunities: Connecting with peers in your industry can provide insights into common financial challenges and how others are overcoming them.
- Access to Industry-Specific Financial Resources: Many associations offer resources like financial planning templates, benchmarking tools, and regulatory updates that are tailored to your industry's unique needs.
- Advocacy and Support: Associations often advocate on behalf of their members on regulatory and policy issues,

providing a collective voice that can influence industry standards and practices.

To get the most out of membership, actively participate in events, join committees, or even offer to speak at conferences. It's about contributing to the community as much as it is about benefiting from it.

Creating Peer Support Groups

Sometimes, the most valuable advice comes from those who are walking the same path as you. Peer support groups, whether formal or informal, offer a platform for sharing experiences, challenges, and successes. Here's how to create or find such a group:

- Local Business Meetups: Sites like Meetup.com can help you find or start a local group of small business owners. These meetups can be invaluable for sharing localized advice and resources.
- Online Groups: Social media platforms like LinkedIn and Facebook host numerous groups for small business owners. These can be great for asking questions, sharing experiences, and staying abreast of industry trends.
- Mastermind Groups: More structured than casual meetups, mastermind groups involve a small number of business owners committed to mutual growth. These groups often meet regularly to set goals, offer feedback, and hold each other accountable.

The key to a successful support group is mutual respect and a shared commitment to growth. Set clear expectations from the outset and foster an environment where members feel comfortable sharing openly.

Building a financial support network is about more than just having experts on speed dial. It's about cultivating relationships with advisors, peers, and industry professionals who can offer guidance, support, and insights that propel your business forward. From identifying key advisors and leveraging online resources to joining industry associations and creating peer support groups, each step strengthens your network, providing a foundation upon which your business can thrive amidst financial challenges and opportunities alike.

9.5 FOSTERING FINANCIAL RESILIENCE: PREPARING FOR THE UNEXPECTED

In the unpredictable dance of running a small business, the music can change at any moment. One day, you're moving smoothly to a jazz rhythm, and the next, you're trying to keep up with a rapid salsa beat. It's in these swift changes of pace that the true resilience of a business is tested. Building financial resilience isn't just about surviving these unexpected shifts; it's about moving through them with grace and coming out stronger on the other side.

Establishing Emergency Funds

Imagine facing a sudden market downturn or an unforeseen expense without a safety net. An emergency fund acts as this safety net, providing a buffer that allows your business to weather financial storms. Start small, aiming to cover at least one month of operating expenses, and gradually build from there. This fund should be easily accessible but separate from your operating accounts to avoid the temptation of dipping into it for day-to-day expenses.

Diversifying Revenue Streams

Relying on a single source of income is like walking a tightrope without a safety harness. Diversification, in contrast, offers a more stable footing. It might mean offering new products or services, exploring different markets, or finding complementary revenue sources such as online courses or merchandise. Each new stream adds a layer of protection, ensuring that if one area faces challenges, your business can continue to thrive on the strength of others.

Risk Management Planning

Every business faces risks, but only some businesses are prepared for them. A comprehensive risk management plan identifies potential risks, evaluates their likelihood and potential impact, and outlines strategies to mitigate them. This plan could cover a wide range of risks, from financial and operational to reputational and compliance-related. Regularly updating this plan ensures it evolves with your business and the external environment, keeping you one step ahead of potential challenges.

- Identify potential risks: Start with a brainstorming session involving your team. Consider everything from natural disasters to cyber-attacks.
- Assess and prioritize: Not all risks carry the same weight. Evaluate each risk based on its potential impact and the likelihood of it occurring.
- Develop mitigation strategies: For the most critical risks, outline specific actions to reduce their likelihood or lessen their impact.

Learning from the Unexpected

Sometimes, despite all the planning, the unexpected still hits. It's in these moments that resilience is truly forged. Reflecting on these experiences provides invaluable insights into your business's vulnerabilities and strengths, offering lessons that can inform future strategies and decisions. Did your team adapt quickly to a sudden shift to remote work? What changes in consumer behavior did you observe during economic fluctuations? Each answer adds a piece of knowledge, contributing to a more resilient and agile business approach.

- Document lessons learned: After navigating a challenge, take the time to document what worked, what didn't, and why. This record becomes a resource for future planning.
- Adapt and evolve: Use these lessons to refine your strategies, processes, and plans, ensuring your business is better prepared for similar situations in the future.

Navigating the unpredictable currents of business requires more than just a good sense of balance; it demands a proactive approach to building financial resilience. From establishing emergency funds as a safety net and diversifying revenue streams to reduce vulnerability to crafting a comprehensive risk management plan and learning from every unexpected twist and turn, these strategies form the cornerstone of a business that not only survives but thrives, no matter what the world throws its way.

As we close this discussion on fostering financial resilience, remember that the goal is to prepare for the unexpected and embrace it as an opportunity for growth and learning. This resilience positions your business for long-term success, ready to face whatever challenges come with confidence and agility. Let's turn our attention to the next chapter, where we'll explore innovative ways to leverage technology, further strengthening your business's financial foundation and ensuring its continued growth and success.

10

NAVIGATING THE DIGITAL WAVE: E-COMMERCE ESSENTIALS FOR SMALL BUSINESSES

I magine walking into a bustling market; the air is thick with the aroma of freshly brewed coffee, chatter fills the space, and every stall is a mini-universe, offering everything from hand-crafted jewelry to vintage books. Now, picture translating this vibrant market scene into the digital world. That's e-commerce for small businesses—a boundless marketplace where your products or services can reach customers far beyond your local area.

10.1 INTRODUCTION TO E-COMMERCE FOR SMALL BUSINESSES

As more consumers flock online for their shopping needs, the growth of e-commerce isn't just impressive; it's reshaping the retail landscape. Small businesses are finding a vast, new playing field, from the mom-and-pop shops to the artisans and service providers. But with great opportunity comes the challenge of integrating this digital storefront with your bookkeeping practices. Let's dive into why this integration is beneficial and necessary for your e-commerce success.

Overview of E-Commerce Growth Trends

- Soaring Sales: It's no secret that e-commerce sales have continued upward. This isn't a fleeting trend; it's the future of retail. Small businesses, from boutique clothing stores to specialty food producers, are expanding their reach and boosting sales by tapping into online markets.
- Changing Consumer Behavior: Today's consumers value convenience, variety, and the ability to shop from the comfort of their homes. E-commerce meets these expectations head-on, offering 24/7 shopping experiences that brick-and-mortar stores can't match.
- Technological Advances: The evolution of technology has lowered the barriers to entry for small businesses to establish an online presence. From user-friendly e-commerce platforms to sophisticated payment processing solutions, setting up shop online has always been challenging.

Importance of Integrating E-Commerce with Bookkeeping

- Real-Time Financial Visibility: Integrating your e-commerce operations with bookkeeping software gives you a real-time view of your financial health. This means you can make informed decisions quickly, whether restocking a best-selling product or adjusting your marketing strategy.
- Streamlined Operations: Manual data entry is time-consuming and prone to errors. When your e-commerce platform talks directly to your bookkeeping system, it automates the flow of sales data, inventory levels, and expenses, streamlining your operations and freeing up time to focus on growth.

- Tax Compliance Made Easy: E-commerce can complicate tax obligations, especially with sales tax. An integrated bookkeeping system can help manage these complexities, ensuring you collect the correct sales tax amount and making tax time less stressful.
- Informed Inventory Management: Understanding which products are flying off the digital shelves and which ones are lagging is crucial. With e-commerce and bookkeeping integration, you have instant access to sales data and inventory levels, helping you manage stock more effectively and reduce holding costs.

This integration isn't just a back-office upgrade; it's a strategic move that can enhance customer satisfaction, improve financial management, and drive business growth. As you navigate the digital wave, remember that the backbone of a successful e-commerce operation isn't just the products you sell or the marketing strategies you deploy—it's also about how effectively you manage the financial data that flows in and out of your business each day.

With these foundational insights into e-commerce and its significance for small businesses, you can leverage the digital marketplace better. Consider these trends and integration benefits while exploring setting up or expanding your e-commerce presence. The digital market is vast and full of opportunities; small businesses can survive and thrive in this exciting space with the right strategies and tools.

10.2 SETTING UP AN E-COMMERCE BUSINESS

The adventure into e-commerce is much like opening a physical store in the digital realm. The storefront is your website, the aisles are your product categories, and the checkout is your payment gateway. Yet, setting up shop online involves decisions that can significantly impact both your sales and how you handle your finances. Two critical elements at this stage are selecting a good e-commerce platform and understanding the nuances of payment processing options.

Choosing the Right E-commerce Platform

Picking a platform is the first step in crafting your online store. This choice influences not only the aesthetics and functionality of your shop but also the operational aspects like inventory management, marketing tools, and, importantly, the integration with bookkeeping software.

- User Experience: Your platform should offer a seamless shopping experience for your customers, with intuitive navigation and fast loading times. A satisfied customer is more likely to return and recommend your store to others.
- Scalability: As your business grows, your platform needs to accommodate increased traffic and more complex inventory without hiccups. Opt for a solution that grows with you, preventing the need for costly migrations later on.
- Integration Capabilities: Ensure the platform can easily connect with other tools and services, especially your bookkeeping software. This connectivity is vital for automating financial tasks and maintaining accurate records.

- Cost: Analyze the total cost of ownership, including monthly fees, transaction charges, and any additional costs for plugins or extensions. It's about balancing the features you need and what you can afford.
- Support and Community: Access to reliable customer support and a vibrant community of users can be invaluable, especially in the early days when you're still finding your way around.

Making an informed choice involves weighing these factors against your current needs and future goals. It's advisable to test drive a few platforms through free trials to get a hands-on feel for what works best for your business.

Payment Processing Options and Their Bookkeeping Implications

Once your store is up, you need to be able to accept payments. The right payment gateway facilitates this, acting as the intermediary that securely transfers money from your customer's account to yours. Yet, the gateway choice influences more than just the transaction process; it affects how sales data flows into your bookkeeping system.

- Ease of Integration: A gateway that integrates seamlessly with your e-commerce platform and bookkeeping software simplifies the recording of sales, taxes, and fees. Look for options that offer direct plugins or APIs for your chosen e-commerce and bookkeeping platforms.
- Transaction Fees: Every payment processor charges fees, which can vary widely. These fees need to be recorded accurately as business expenses in your bookkeeping system. Opting for a payment processor with transparent,

competitive pricing and straightforward fee structures can make this process easier and more predictable.

- Security and Compliance: Ensuring the safe handling of customer data is paramount. Choose a payment processor that complies with the Payment Card Industry Data Security Standard (PCI DSS). This protects your customers and shields your business from potential liabilities and fines.

- Payment Methods: Offering various payment options can increase conversions by allowing customers to use their preferred method. Each option, from credit cards to digital wallets, comes with its own fees and processing times, all of which need to be tracked and recorded in your financial systems.

- Reconciliation Features: Some payment processors provide tools that simplify the reconciliation process, matching transactions with bank statements and ensuring that your bookkeeping records are accurate. This feature can save significant time and reduce errors in your financial reporting.

Integrating your payment processing system and bookkeeping software is a critical puzzle piece. It ensures that every sale, refund, and fee is automatically recorded, providing you with up-to-date financial insights. This automation not only streamlines your operations but also provides a solid foundation for financial analysis, helping you make informed decisions about the future of your business.

In navigating the setup of your e-commerce business, your choices in selecting a platform and payment processing options lay the groundwork for your operational efficiency and financial clarity. Each decision should be approached with an eye toward immediate needs, long-term growth, and scalability. With the right tools and systems, you can focus more on growing your business and less on the intricacies of online sales and bookkeeping.

10.3 E-COMMERCE SALES AND BOOKKEEPING

In e-commerce, the influx of daily transactions, from a whirlwind of sales to the constant drip of expenses and fees, creates a dynamic financial environment that small business owners must navigate with precision and foresight. This section dives into the methods and practices that ensure accurate tracking and management of online sales, expenses, and the ever-important task of sales tax collection and remittance.

Keeping a Pulse on Online Sales

The digital storefront operates round the clock, bringing in sales data that needs to be meticulously recorded and analyzed. The key to staying on top of this data flow lies in setting up a system that not only captures every transaction but also categorizes and stores this information in an easily retrievable manner. Here's how:

- Automated Sales Tracking: Utilizing e-commerce platforms that integrate directly with your bookkeeping software can automate the capture of sales data. This setup ensures that each sale and its corresponding customer and product information flows directly into your financial records, eliminating the need for manual data entry and reducing the risk of errors.
- Daily Reconciliation: Implementing a daily practice of reconciling your sales transactions with your bank deposits can highlight discrepancies early on. This routine encourages a proactive approach to financial management,

ensuring that your records accurately reflect your business's cash flow.

- Segmentation of Revenue Streams: If your e-commerce business operates across multiple channels or offers a diverse range of products, segmenting your revenue streams in your bookkeeping system can provide valuable insights. This segmentation allows you to track the performance of different aspects of your business, identifying trends and making informed decisions about where to focus your growth efforts.

Managing E-commerce Expenses and Fees

Beyond the glow of sales numbers, e-commerce operations incur various expenses and fees, from platform subscription costs to payment processing fees. A clear strategy for tracking and managing these expenses is crucial for maintaining healthy profit margins. Here's a strategy tailored to address this need:

- Categorization of Expenses: Assigning each expense to a specific category within your bookkeeping system simplifies tracking and analyzing your operational costs. This categorization can range from marketing expenses and subscription fees to shipping costs and payment processing charges.
- Regular Expense Review: Establishing a routine for reviewing your e-commerce expenses lets you identify areas where costs can be optimized. Whether negotiating better rates with suppliers or switching to a payment processor with lower fees, small adjustments can lead to significant savings over time.
- Budget Allocation: Setting a budget for your e-commerce operations and regularly comparing actual expenses

against this budget can help you stay on track. This practice encourages disciplined spending and can highlight areas where your business may be over or under-investing.

Sales Tax Collection and Remittance

The collection and remittance of sales tax present a unique challenge in the e-commerce landscape, where transactions often cross state and international boundaries. Navigating this complex terrain requires a thoughtful approach:

- Understanding Tax Jurisdictions: Familiarizing yourself with the sales tax laws of the states and countries where you operate is the first step. Many e-commerce platforms offer tools that automatically calculate the appropriate sales tax based on the customer's location, simplifying this process.
- Automating Tax Collection: Leveraging features within your e-commerce platform that automatically apply the correct sales tax rate at checkout ensures you collect the right amount from each sale. This automation can relieve you of a significant administrative burden.
- Timely Tax Remittance: Establishing a calendar for sales tax remittance, aligned with the deadlines set by the relevant tax authorities, is essential. Bookkeeping software that tracks sales tax collected and reminders for upcoming remittance deadlines helps ensure you never miss a payment.
- Record-Keeping for Audits: Maintaining detailed records of all sales transactions, including the amount of sales tax collected and remitted, prepares you for potential audits. These records should be easily accessible within your

bookkeeping system, ensuring you can quickly retrieve them if required by a tax authority.

Navigating the financial intricacies of e-commerce requires a keen understanding of sales, expenses, and tax obligations and a commitment to leveraging technology and best practices in financial management. By automating data capture, diligently tracking and reviewing expenses, and adhering to sales tax regulations, you can create a robust financial framework for your e-commerce business. This framework supports operational efficiency and compliance and provides the insights to drive strategic decisions and foster sustainable growth.

10.4 INVENTORY MANAGEMENT FOR E-COMMERCE

Managing inventory effectively is similar to the delicate balance of ensuring enough coffee to serve every morning rush without ending up with surplus beans that lose their freshness. For e-commerce businesses, this equilibrium is vital. Not only does it prevent stock outs that could lead to missed sales, but it also avoids excess inventory that ties up capital and storage space. Here, we delve into strategies and tools that sharpen your approach to inventory management, turning it into a smooth, well-oiled machine that supports both customer satisfaction and financial health.

Best Practices in Inventory Tracking

Tracking inventory goes beyond knowing how many items are on the shelf; it's about understanding sales patterns, predicting demand, and preparing for fluctuations. These practices lay the groundwork for effective inventory management:

- SKU Management: Assign a unique Stock Keeping Unit (SKU) to each product variant. This coding system allows you to precisely track sales and inventory levels, making it easier to identify which items are performing well and which aren't.
- Regular Audits: While digital tools offer a real-time glimpse into inventory levels, physical counts are indispensable. Schedule regular audits to compare what's on the books versus what's actually in stock. Discrepancies can indicate issues like theft, damage, or data entry errors.
- Supplier Performance Tracking: Keep tabs on how well your suppliers meet their commitments. Delays or inconsistencies can disrupt your inventory flow and, consequently, your ability to fulfill orders. Evaluating supplier performance helps in making informed decisions about future partnerships.
- Demand Forecasting: Use historical sales data to predict future demand, adjusting for seasonality, marketing campaigns, and industry trends. This foresight allows you to stock up, anticipating increased demand, ensuring you're never caught off guard.
- Safety Stock Levels: Determine the minimum quantity of each product that should always be on hand to cover unexpected spikes in demand or delays in restocking. This safety stock acts as a buffer, preventing stockouts.

Implementing these practices requires diligent monitoring, data analysis, and proactive planning. As you refine your approach, you'll find your business better positioned to respond to market dynamics, maintain optimal inventory levels, and meet customer expectations consistently.

Automated Inventory Management Tools

The evolution of inventory management has been significantly influenced by technology, with automated tools now available to streamline every aspect of the process. These tools can transform inventory management from a potential headache into a strategic advantage:

- Cloud-Based Inventory Management Systems: Platforms like Shopify, WooCommerce, and BigCommerce offer integrated inventory management solutions that sync with your e-commerce store. Real-time updates ensure that sales on any channel adjust inventory levels accordingly, preventing overselling and stockouts.
- Barcode Scanning: Tools that support barcode scanning simplify adding new products to your inventory and updating quantities. This method reduces the chances of human error during data entry and speeds up receiving new stock and fulfilling orders.
- Automated Reordering: Set reordering thresholds within your inventory management system to automatically generate purchase orders when stock levels fall below a specified point. This automation ensures that you're always poised to replenish your inventory in time, keeping pace with demand.
- Dropshipping Integration: For businesses that use dropshipping, integrating with your suppliers' systems can automate order fulfillment. When a customer orders on your site, the details are directly sent to the supplier, who then ships the product on your behalf. This model minimizes the need for physical inventory, freeing up resources for other aspects of your business.

- Analytics and Reporting: Advanced inventory management systems offer analytics features that analyze sales patterns, track bestsellers, and identify slow-moving items. These insights guide inventory decisions, from adjusting product lines to optimizing stock levels for peak efficiency.

Choosing the right tools involves evaluating your business's needs, budget, and growth plans. By harnessing the power of automation, you can elevate your inventory management, ensuring it supports your current operations and scales with your business as it grows. This strategic approach to inventory management bolsters your e-commerce venture, aligning stock levels with market demand, optimizing storage and capital use, and ultimately enhancing customer satisfaction through reliable order fulfillment. With the right practices and tools, inventory management becomes a cornerstone of your business's operational excellence and financial health, driving sustainable growth in the competitive e-commerce landscape.

10.5 E-COMMERCE REPORTING AND ANALYSIS

In the digital marketplace, success often hinges on interpreting and acting on the correct data. E-commerce reporting and analysis equip you with the insights to refine your strategy, optimize operations, and, ultimately, drive business growth. This segment unfolds the layers of e-commerce metrics that matter and how to employ this data to amplify your business's performance.

Grasping E-commerce Metrics

At the heart of e-commerce, many metrics pulse with information, each telling a story about different facets of your business. While the vast array of data available can seem daunting, focusing on key metrics can illuminate the path to enhanced performance and profitability:

- **Conversion Rate:** This metric offers insights into the effectiveness of your website and marketing efforts by showing the percentage of visitors who make a purchase. Improving this rate often involves refining your site's user experience and tailoring marketing messages.

Conversion rate formula = Conversions / Total visitors x 100

- *Conversion rate example:*

A retail shop specializing in posters finds that out of 12,355 site visitors, 181 purchased concert posters. Using the basic conversion rate formula, you find that your site experienced a 1.46% conversion rate for poster sales:

$$181 / 12,355 = 0.014649940.01464994 \times 100 = 1.46499393 = 1.46\%$$

- **Average Order Value (AOV):** By understanding the typical spend per transaction, you can strategize ways to encourage customers to add more to their carts, possibly through product recommendations or bundled offers.

Average Order Value formula = Revenue / Number of orders

- *Average Order Value example:*

An e-commerce store for Q3 has the following financial data: the store earned $100,000 in revenue from 2,000 orders. Using the basic average order value formula, you find that your store had an AOV of $50:

$$\$100,000 / 2,000 = \$50$$

- **Customer Lifetime Value (CLV):** This indicator predicts the total value a customer will bring to your business throughout their relationship with you. Increasing CLV can be achieved by enhancing customer satisfaction and implementing loyalty programs.

Customer Lifetime Value formula = Average order value × Number of transactions × Average length of the customer relationship (in years)

- *Average Lifetime Value example:*

Grocery stores inspire loyalty among residents within the vicinity. Let's say a shopper frequents a grocery in New York every week. He spends around $100 per visit. He returned every week, 52 weeks a year, for an average of three years.

$100 (purchase per visit) × 52 (visits per year) × 3 (years) = $15,600 (CLV)

- **Cart Abandonment Rate:** A high rate might signal checkout or pricing transparency issues. Addressing these can significantly boost sales.

Cart Abandonment Rate formula = 1- total completed purchases / # of shopping carts created x 100

- *Cart Abandonment Rate example:*

An online store has 45 completed purchases and 200 shopping carts created. The shopping cart abandonment rate would be 77.5%.

$$1 - (45 / 200) \times 100 = 77.5\%$$

- **Traffic Sources:** Identifying which channels drive visitors to your site lets you focus your marketing efforts and budget on the most effective platforms.

By keeping a steady eye on these metrics, you better understand where your e-commerce business stands and where it could go.

Using Data for Business Growth

The true power of e-commerce metrics lies in their application. With the right approach, the data harvested from your online store can become the catalyst for growth and expansion. Here's how to navigate through the sea of data towards actionable insights:

- Segment and Target: Break down your data to understand the behaviors and preferences of different customer segments. Tailored marketing efforts can more effectively reach and resonate with each group, improving conversion rates and customer retention.
- Optimize Marketing Spend: By analyzing the return on investment (ROI) of different marketing channels, you can allocate your budget more effectively, focusing on the avenues that yield the best results.
- Enhance Product Offerings: Sales data and customer feedback highlight which products hit and which missed

the mark. This insight guides product development and inventory decisions, ensuring you invest in lines that meet your customers' needs and desires.

- Personalize the Customer Experience: Leveraging data on customer preferences and purchasing history allows for personalized experiences, from tailored product recommendations to customized marketing messages. This level of personalization can significantly uplift AOV and CLV.
- Streamline Operations: From pinpointing bottlenecks in the fulfillment process to identifying inefficiencies in customer service, data analysis can uncover opportunities to streamline operations, reduce costs, and improve customer satisfaction.

Essentially, the strategic application of e-commerce metrics can transform raw data into a business optimization and growth roadmap. It empowers you to make informed decisions, adapt to market trends, and meet your customers' evolving needs with precision and agility.

As we wrap up this exploration of e-commerce reporting and analysis, it becomes clear that the key to thriving in the digital marketplace lies in understanding and leveraging the wealth of data at your fingertips. By focusing on crucial metrics and employing this data to refine your strategy and operations, you unlock the potential for sustained growth and profitability. This journey through the digital marketplace continues, with each data point serving as a beacon, guiding your decisions and strategies in an ever-evolving landscape.

The insights gleaned from your e-commerce reporting are not just numbers on a page. They are the pulse of your business, the indicators of your success, and the guideposts for your future strategies. The following chapter will explore how to structure your small business, setting the stage for even greater achievements in your business venture.

11

TAILORING YOUR FINANCIAL FABRIC: UNDERSTANDING BUSINESS STRUCTURES

Picture this: You're at a sprawling buffet, each dish offering a different blend of flavors, nutrients, and culinary experiences. Deciding what to put on your plate can feel overwhelming. Similarly, when standing at the threshold of your entrepreneurial venture, choosing the right business structure is like navigating this buffet. Each structure offers its unique blend of legal protections, tax implications, and operational flexibilities. This chapter aims to simplify this selection process, much like choosing your meal, by breaking down the complexities into digestible parts.

11.1 INTRODUCTION TO BUSINESS STRUCTURES

Overview of Common Business Structures

Navigating the world of business structures can feel like trying to find your way through a dense forest without a map. Here's a flashlight to guide you through:

- Sole Proprietorships: Imagine running a lemonade stand in your front yard. You're the boss, the employee, and the finance department all rolled into one. This is the essence of a sole proprietorship. It's just you running the show, enjoying all the profits, and bearing all the losses and responsibilities.
- Partnerships: Now, imagine your friend joining you at your lemonade stand. You agree to share profits, losses, and decision-making. This arrangement is a partnership. It's a simple way to pool resources and share the journey, but remember, you're also sharing the responsibility for any debts and decisions your partner makes.
- Limited Liability Companies (LLCs): Consider this as your lemonade stand evolving. You're still in charge, but now you have a safety net. Your personal assets are generally protected from business debts if things go south. Plus, you get a say in how you're taxed, which can be a sweet deal.
- S Corporations: This is your lemonade stand joining the big leagues. You can still protect your personal assets, but now there's a cap on the Number of shareholders you can have. The real cherry on top is that you can save on self-employment taxes, though the paperwork can get hefty.
- C Corporations: Imagine your lemonade stand turning into a franchise. It's an entirely separate entity from you, the owner. This structure can go public, sell stocks, and be taxed separately. It's the most complex but offers significant growth potential and protection.

Key Differences in Liability, Taxation, and Ownership

Choosing between these structures is more than just a matter of preference; it's about aligning with your business goals, financial situation, and how much risk you're willing to take. Here's a closer look:

- Liability: Sole proprietors and partners are like acrobats without a net; they are personally responsible for business debts. LLCs, S Corporations, and C Corporations throw a safety net under you, limiting your risk.
- Taxation: If you dislike paperwork, sole proprietorships, and partnerships, keep it simple; profits and losses pass through to your individual tax return. LLCs offer flexibility; you choose how you're taxed. S and C Corporations are more complex, each with its own tax benefits and obligations.
- Ownership: Sole proprietorships and single-member LLCs are solo acts. Partnerships, multi-member LLCs, and S Corporations are more of a band, with multiple members sharing control. C Corporations are like orchestras, with potentially many members and a more structured leadership.

Understanding these differences is crucial. It's not just about where you are now but where you see your business in the future. Choosing the right structure can save money, protect your assets, and set you up for success.

Visual Element: Chart Comparing Business Structures

To help visualize these differences, see the chart below with columns for each business structure and rows for formation, liability, taxation, and ownership. Each cell details how each structure addresses these aspects. For instance, under the "Liability" row, sole proprietorships and partnerships are marked "No" for

Limited personal liability, while LLCs and corporations are showing "Yes" for having Limited personal liability.

	Sole Proprietor	Partnership	C Corp	S Corp	Professional Corporation	Nonprofit Corp	Limited Liability Co.
Formation	No filing required	No filing required	State filing required	State filing required	State filing required	State and federal filings required	State filing required
Limited personal liability	No	No	Yes	Yes	Yes, except for own malpractice	Yes	Yes
Transferability of interest	No	No	Yes	Generally limited	Generally limited	N/A	Yes, often limited
Duration	Until withdrawal or death of the owner	Unlimited	Unlimited	Unlimited	Unlimited	Unlimited	Unlimited
Pass-through taxation	Yes	Yes	No	Yes	No	Tax exempt	Yes, upon election
Ability to raise capital	Not as a separate entity	Yes	Yes	Yes, but shareholder limits	Yes	Yes, through donations and grants	Yes
Limitations on the number of owners	Yes	No	No	Yes	No, but all owners must be part of the same profession	N/A	No

Interactive Element: Quiz on Choosing Your Business Structure

Consider a short quiz with scenarios and questions about your business goals, financial situation, and risk tolerance. Your answers could suggest which business structure might fit your needs, offering a personalized touch to this decision-making process. Remember, while this quiz can provide guidance, consulting with a financial advisor or accountant for tailored advice is invaluable.

Understanding the intricacies of business structures isn't just about legal compliance or tax savings; it's about laying a solid foundation for your business's future. Like choosing the right ingredients for a meal, selecting the appropriate structure is about creating the perfect blend that suits your taste, meets your nutritional needs, and fits your lifestyle. With the right structure, you're not just starting a business but setting the stage for your entrepreneurial dreams to flourish.

Sole Proprietorships

Navigating the terrain of sole proprietorships, one finds a path less encumbered by the formalities that shackle more complex business structures. Here, the simplicity of operations isn't just a perk; it's the pulse of the entity, driving its day-to-day activities and strategic decisions. This simplicity extends into bookkeeping and tax preparation, areas often viewed with fear by the unprepared. In sole proprietorships, however, these tasks assume a more approachable demeanor, encouraging even those with minimal financial knowledge to confidently take the reins of their financial affairs.

Simplified Bookkeeping and Tax Preparation

A bookkeeping system that avoids complexity in favor of straightforwardness is at the heart of a sole proprietorship's financial management. Without needing to navigate the intricate financial records of partnerships or corporations, sole proprietors benefit from a streamlined process that focuses on the essentials of tracking income and expenses. This simplicity is mirrored in tax preparation. With business profits and losses flowing directly to the owner's personal tax return, intertwining business and individual taxation simplifies the process, eliminating the need for separate tax filings for the business entity.

204 | D.K. BURNETT

- Direct Tax Reporting: Profits and losses directly impact the proprietor's personal tax situation, simplifying annual tax filings.
- Ease of Record-Keeping: Maintaining accurate records becomes more manageable with fewer transactions and less complex financial activities.

The Importance of Separating Personal and Business Finances

Despite the intertwined nature of personal and business finances in a sole proprietorship, drawing a clear line between the two is paramount. As discussed in the previous chapter, this separation not only aids in financial clarity but also fortifies the business's credibility and professionalism.

Tracking Expenses and Income with a Single-Entry System

For many sole proprietors, the single-entry bookkeeping system offers a fitting solution to their financial tracking needs. Characterized by its simplicity, this system records each financial transaction as a single entry, either as income or an expense. This approach aligns with the straightforward nature of sole proprietorships, where the primary financial activities revolve around receiving payments for services or products sold and paying out for business-related expenses.

- Simplicity and Accessibility: The single-entry system is easily understood, even by those with little to no background in finance, making it accessible to a wide range of business owners.
- Adequate for Basic Financial Management: For businesses with straightforward financial transactions, this system provides sufficient detail for managing finances effectively.

However, it's important to recognize when the business's growth calls for a more sophisticated approach. As transactions increase in volume and complexity, transitioning to a double-entry system might become necessary to capture the nuances of the business's financial activities fully.

In sole proprietorships, the journey through financial management is marked by simplicity and directness. From streamlined bookkeeping and tax preparation processes to maintaining a clear boundary between personal and business finances, these principles serve as guiding lights. The adoption of a single-entry bookkeeping system further underscores this approach, offering a straightforward method for tracking the financial heartbeat of the business. In this landscape, sole proprietors find themselves equipped to navigate their financial responsibilities with clarity and confidence, ensuring their business survives and thrives in the competitive marketplace.

Partnerships

Navigating the financial dynamics of a partnership is like a duo or group performance on stage, where harmony and rhythm are crucial for a stellar presentation. In this setup, partners contribute their unique talents, resources, and investments to create a symphony of business operations to achieve shared goals. However, orchestrating this harmony requires meticulous attention to managing capital accounts, allocating profits and losses, and handling contributions and withdrawals. Each of these elements plays a distinct note in the financial melody of a partnership, contributing to its overall success or failure.

Managing Capital Accounts for Each Partner

In the world of partnerships, a capital account represents a ledger for each partner, documenting their contribution to the firm. Think of it as a personal scorecard that tracks what each partner brings to the business table, including initial investments, additional funds, and the share of profits retained in the business.

- Initial Contributions: When the partnership forms, each partner's initial investment, whether in cash, property, or services, is recorded in their respective capital account. This sets the foundation for equity distribution among partners.
- Ongoing Contributions and Distributions: Partners might inject more capital or withdraw funds for personal use as the business evolves. These transactions are meticulously tracked in the capital account, ensuring transparency and trust among partners.
- Reflecting Ownership Stake: The balance in a partner's capital account often reflects their ownership stake in the partnership, influencing decision-making power and profit-sharing ratios.

Adjustments to these accounts are made regularly, capturing the ebb and flow of contributions and withdrawals. This fluidity requires a system that maintains accuracy and offers clarity to all partners involved, ensuring each member is fairly credited for their share of the investment and profits.

Allocating Profits and Losses According to the Partnership Agreement

The heartbeat of a partnership's financial health lies in its ability to generate profits. However, the rhythm can fluctuate, leading to periods of loss. Similar to a musical score, the partnership agreement outlines how these profits and losses are divided among partners.

- Predetermined Ratios: Often, the agreement specifies ratios for dividing profits and losses, reflecting each partner's contribution, risk appetite, and agreed-upon expectations. This method promotes fairness and reduces conflicts.
- Special Allocations: There might be clauses for special allocations, where certain profits or losses are assigned to specific partners based on unique contributions or for tax optimization purposes.
- Flexibility and Adaptation: The agreement allows for adjustments, accommodating changes in the partnership dynamics, business growth, or shifts in individual partner roles.

This allocation process ensures that each partner receives their fair share of the bounty or bears their portion of the burden, reinforcing the partnership's foundation based on equity and mutual respect.

Handling Partner Contributions and Withdrawals

The fluid nature of a partnership means that partners might periodically contribute additional capital or withdraw funds for personal use. These movements are akin to the improvisational solos in a musical performance, where flexibility and personal expression are essential.

- Documenting Contributions: Additional contributions, whether in cash, property, or services, are recorded in the partner's capital account. This increases their stake in the partnership, potentially altering profit-sharing ratios and decision-making influence.
- Regulating Withdrawals: Withdrawals by partners, often called draws, are carefully recorded and deducted from the partner's capital account. While these withdrawals provide partners with liquidity, they must be managed to ensure the partnership retains sufficient capital for operations and growth.
- Agreement Provisions: The partnership agreement often sets guidelines for contributions and withdrawals, including limits, timing, and procedures, to maintain financial stability and harmony among partners.

This dance of contributions and withdrawals requires a keen eye on the partnership's liquidity and long-term financial goals, ensuring that individual partner needs are balanced with the collective objectives of the firm.

In partnerships, the interplay between managing capital accounts, allocating profits and losses, and handling contributions and withdrawals forms a complex financial choreography that demands precision, transparency, and harmony. Each partner plays a crucial role in this dance, contributing their unique strengths and resources towards the partnership's success. The meticulous management of these financial aspects ensures that the partnership remains on solid ground, poised for growth, and able to navigate the challenges and opportunities that lie ahead.

Limited Liability Companies (LLCs)

Stepping into the arena of Limited Liability Companies (LLCs) introduces a level of flexibility and protection that many entrepreneurs find appealing. The allure of LLCs lies in their unique ability to blend the simplicity of sole proprietorships and partnerships with the liability protections of corporations. This hybrid structure is particularly beneficial for small to medium-sized businesses seeking operational flexibility without the formalities of a corporation. One of the most significant advantages of an LLC is its adaptable approach to taxation, allowing members to select the tax status that best suits their financial goals.

Flexibility in Tax Treatment

At its core, the tax structure of an LLC is designed for adaptability. Unlike other business entities with a fixed tax status, an LLC can be taxed as a disregarded entity, partnership, or corporation. By default, single-member LLCs are taxed similarly to sole proprietorships, and multi-member LLCs, like partnerships, with profits and losses passing through to the members' personal tax returns. However, if it's financially advantageous, an LLC can elect to be taxed as either an S Corporation or a C Corporation, bringing about potential savings in self-employment taxes and providing an opportunity for income splitting among members.

- **Disregarded Entity:** For single-member LLCs, this default status allows for direct reporting of profits and losses on the owner's personal tax return, simplifying the tax filing process.
- **Partnership:** Multi-member LLCs naturally fall into this category, where the company itself doesn't pay taxes.

Instead, profits are passed through to members, who report them on their personal returns.

- **Corporation Election:** Both single and multi-member LLCs can opt for corporate tax status, offering a strategic avenue for tax planning, especially regarding potentially lower corporate tax rates and eligibility for certain deductions.

Capital Account Management and Member Distributions

Managing the capital accounts in an LLC involves tracking each member's contributions, share of profits, and withdrawals. Just as each member brings unique resources to the business, their capital accounts reflect their ongoing financial relationship with the company. These accounts are crucial for understanding the financial standing of each member within the LLC and serve as a record for determining the distribution of profits and the handling of losses.

- Initial Contributions: Recorded at the start, these set the baseline for each member's equity in the LLC.
- Ongoing Activity: Regular contributions and distributions are tracked, adjusting each member's equity in real time.
- Profit Distribution: Profits can be distributed according to the operating agreement, which might not always align with the percentage of ownership, offering flexibility in financial planning.

Proper management of these accounts is vital for ensuring fairness and transparency among members, serving as a cornerstone for the financial health and stability of the LLC.

Bookkeeping Considerations for Multi-Member LLCs vs. Single-Member LLCs

Navigating bookkeeping for LLCs requires a tailored approach, especially when comparing the needs of single-member entities to those with multiple members. For single-member LLCs, the simplicity of their structure allows for a more straightforward bookkeeping process, similar to that of a sole proprietorship but with the added benefit of limited liability. The primary focus is accurately recording all business transactions, maintaining clear separation from personal finances, and preparing for seamless tax reporting under the disregarded entity status.

Multi-member LLCs encounter a more complex financial landscape. The collective nature of these entities necessitates a comprehensive bookkeeping strategy that encompasses:

- Individual Capital Accounts: Detailed records of each member's financial interactions with the LLC are essential for maintaining transparency and equity.
- Profit and Loss Allocation: Accurate tracking of the business's financial performance is crucial for equitable distribution of profits and assignment of losses, per the operating agreement.
- Inter-member Transactions: Any financial exchanges between members and the LLC, outside of regular distributions, must be meticulously documented to ensure clarity and prevent disputes.

For single and multi-member LLCs, employing a double-entry bookkeeping system elevates the accuracy of financial records. This method ensures that for every transaction, corresponding entries are made to reflect the movement of resources, providing a

212 | D.K. BURNETT

complete picture of the business's financial health. Additionally, leveraging bookkeeping software that caters to the needs of LLCs can streamline financial management, automate tax preparation, and facilitate reporting, allowing members to focus more on growth and less on administrative tasks.

Navigating the financial intricacies of LLCs, from tax treatment and capital account management to tailored bookkeeping practices, underscores the importance of a strategic approach to financial management. By understanding and leveraging the unique benefits of the LLC structure, entrepreneurs can protect their interests, optimize their tax situation, and lay a strong foundation for the future success of their ventures.

S Corporations

Embracing the structure of an S Corporation brings its unique set of financial nuances, particularly in the realms of payroll processing, shareholder compensation, and tax considerations. This business format, often chosen for its blend of liability protection and tax benefits, demands a meticulous approach to managing its finances. This section highlights these critical areas, ensuring clarity and compliance for S Corporation owners.

Payroll Processing and Reasonable Compensation for Shareholders

One of the pivotal aspects of financial management within an S Corporation revolves around payroll. Unlike sole proprietors or partners in a partnership, who may directly draw from the business's profits, shareholders in an S Corporation must receive reasonable compensation through payroll for their services. This requirement means:

- Setting Up a Formal Payroll System: This allows the business to process salaries, withhold the appropriate taxes, and contribute to employment taxes. The system ensures that all financial obligations regarding employee compensation are met promptly and accurately.
- Determining Reasonable Compensation: The IRS scrutinizes the compensation paid to shareholder-employees to ensure it reflects the fair market value for their roles. Factors influencing this determination include the shareholder's responsibilities, the hours worked, and comparable salaries within the same industry.
- Benefits of Payroll: While handling payroll adds an extra layer of operational complexity, it also clearly delineates the profits distributed to shareholders and the compensation for their active involvement in the business. This distinction is crucial for tax reporting and can offer advantages in reducing self-employment taxes.

Documenting Shareholder Distributions and Stock Basis

In addition to receiving compensation through payroll, shareholders in an S Corporation might receive distributions from the business's profits. Managing and documenting these distributions requires attention to detail for several reasons:

- Stock Basis Calculation: Shareholders need to maintain an accurate record of their stock basis, which is essentially their investment in the corporation. This basis gets adjusted annually based on the shareholder's share of the corporation's income, losses, and distributions. It's crucial for determining the tax implications of any distributions received over and above the shareholder's compensation.

- Non-Dividend Distributions: Typically, distributions are not subject to tax if they do not exceed the shareholder's stock basis. However, distributions that exceed this basis may be taxable as capital gains. Keeping meticulous records of these transactions is essential for accurate tax reporting.
- Annual Adjustments: The stock basis is not static; it requires yearly adjustments that account for the shareholder's proportionate share of the corporation's income, losses, and deductions. This ongoing adjustment process underlines the corporation's importance of consistent and detailed financial documentation.

Special Tax Considerations and Benefits

The S Corporation structure offers tax advantages that can be leveraged with careful planning and compliance. Key among these are:

- Pass-Through Taxation: Similar to partnerships and LLCs, S Corporations enjoy pass-through taxation, where income is reported on the shareholders' personal tax returns, avoiding the double taxation faced by C Corporations. This structure can lead to potential tax savings, especially when combined with strategic payroll and distribution planning.
- Self-Employment Tax Savings: By splitting income between reasonable compensation (subject to employment taxes) and distributions (not subject to employment taxes), shareholder-employees can potentially lower their overall tax burden. However, this strategy requires a balanced approach to ensure compliance with IRS guidelines for reasonable compensation.

- Fringe Benefits: Certain fringe benefits provided to shareholder-employees, such as health insurance premiums paid by the corporation, can be deducted by the corporation and are tax-free to the employee up to the extent of their stock basis. This arrangement provides an additional avenue for tax-efficient compensation planning.

Navigating the financial intricacies of S Corporations involves:

- A careful balance between leveraging the tax benefits.
- Ensuring compliance with payroll and compensation requirements.
- Maintaining accurate records of shareholder transactions.

By focusing on these critical areas, owners can optimize their tax positions, protect their assets, and set a solid foundation for their business's financial health. While demanding diligence and attention to detail, this approach unlocks the potential for S Corporations to thrive, combining the operational flexibility of a smaller entity with the structural benefits of a corporate form.

C Corporations

The stakes are high in the realm of C Corporations, and the rewards can be substantial. This business structure provides a robust framework for growth, investor attraction, and market expansion but has an intricate web of responsibilities. Among these, maintaining a detailed record for corporate governance stands out as a critical task, acting as both a shield and a strategy for scaling the business. Furthermore, managing payroll and benefits, navigating the labyrinth of tax obligations, and considering double taxation are pivotal aspects that demand meticulous attention.

216 | D.K. BURNETT

Maintaining Comprehensive Records for Corporate Governance

A C Corporation operates under a microscope, with every financial decision and transaction scrutinized by stakeholders and regulatory bodies. In this environment, maintaining comprehensive records goes beyond basic compliance—it becomes a strategic asset. These records encompass minutes from board meetings, shareholder communications, financial statements, and contracts. This meticulous documentation serves multiple purposes:

- It ensures transparency and accountability, reinforcing trust with investors and stakeholders.
- It provides a clear historical account of decisions and transactions, which is invaluable during audits or legal reviews.
- It aids in strategic planning, offering insights into past successes and lessons learned.

For C Corporations, the ledger is not just a book of numbers; it is a narrative of the business's journey, a detailed account that guides future strategies and governance.

Managing Payroll, Benefits, and Dividends

The operational complexity of C Corporations extends into managing payroll and benefits. This task encompasses not just the processing of salaries but also the strategic distribution of benefits that can attract top talent. Here, the corporation must navigate:

- Compliance with federal and state employment laws, ensuring that wages meet minimum standards and that overtime is paid correctly.

- Benefits administration might include health insurance, retirement plans, and stock options. These benefits are not just expenses but investments in employee satisfaction and retention.
- The declaration and payment of dividends to shareholders require a careful balance. While dividends can be a powerful tool for returning value to investors, they must be managed to ensure the corporation retains enough capital for operational needs and growth opportunities.

This intricate dance involves financial acumen and strategic foresight, ensuring the corporation remains competitive and compliant.

Advanced Tax Reporting Requirements and Double Taxation Considerations

One of the most challenging aspects of operating a C Corporation is navigating the complex landscape of tax obligations. The corporation faces a dual layer of taxation: once on its earnings and again at the shareholder level when dividends are paid out. This double taxation scenario demands a strategic approach to tax planning involving:

- Understanding the nuances of corporate tax rates and leveraging deductions and credits to minimize obligations.
- Planning for dividend distributions in a manner that maximizes shareholder value while considering the tax implications for both the corporation and its shareholders.
- Navigating state and federal tax reporting requirements can be complicated, requiring detailed documentation and timely filings.

For C Corporations, tax strategy is not just about compliance; it's about optimizing financial performance and shareholder returns. This requires a deep understanding of tax laws and a proactive approach to financial planning.

The financial landscape is vast and complex in the world of C Corporations. The challenges are significant, from the meticulous documentation required for corporate governance, the strategic management of payroll and benefits, and the nuanced approach needed for tax planning. Yet, with these challenges come opportunities—to grow, innovate, and lead in the marketplace. For C Corporations, success lies in the details and the careful management of the myriad financial duties of this robust business structure.

11.2 CHOOSING THE RIGHT BOOKKEEPING SOFTWARE

In the dynamic landscape of small businesses, selecting the ideal bookkeeping software is akin to picking a seasoned navigator for an uncharted voyage. The right software illuminates the financial path ahead and ensures a smooth journey, adapting to the twists and turns of business growth and evolution. It's about finding a partner that understands the nuances of your business structure, scales with your ambitions, and seamlessly connects with the other tools that keep your business humming.

Tailoring Features to Business Structure

The structure lays the groundwork for every business's operational and financial framework. Your bookkeeping software should mirror this framework, offering features that resonate with your entity's specific needs and challenges.

- Ease of Use for Sole Proprietors: Individuals running their own show need software that simplifies bookkeeping without stripping away power. Look for intuitive interfaces that offer straightforward expense tracking, invoice management, and tax preparation without an overwhelming feature set.

- Collaborative Tools for Partnerships and LLCs: Entities where multiple hands steer the ship benefit from software facilitating collaboration. Essential features include multi-user access, varying permission levels, and real-time updates, ensuring all partners stay informed and engaged with the business's financial health.

- Robust Reporting for S and C Corporations: The complexity of corporate structures demands software with comprehensive reporting capabilities. Detailed financial statements, performance analytics, and shareholder reporting tools are non-negotiable, providing the insights needed to navigate corporate governance and strategic decision-making.

- Tax Compliance Across Structures: Tax compliance remains a universal concern regardless of entity type. The ideal software automates tax calculations, tracks deductible expenses, and integrates with tax filing solutions, simplifying the labyrinth of tax compliance.

As businesses evolve, so do their bookkeeping needs. Software that fits like a glove today must stretch to accommodate tomorrow's growth.

Recommendations for Each Type of Entity

In the vast sea of bookkeeping software options, finding the one that best suits your business structure can be daunting. Here are some tailored recommendations to guide your selection:

- For Sole Proprietors: Consider software that balances simplicity with functionality. Options like FreshBooks and QuickBooks Self-Employed provide an excellent starting point, offering easy-to-navigate interfaces coupled with powerful features tailored to the needs of solo entrepreneurs.
- For Partnerships and LLCs: Software that supports multi-user collaboration and offers flexible reporting is vital. With its comprehensive user permissions and extensive integration capabilities, Xero stands out as a robust solution for businesses operated by multiple partners or members.
- For S Corporations: Look for software that can handle payroll processing and shareholder reporting intricacies. Gusto, integrated with bookkeeping solutions like QuickBooks Online, offers a seamless experience, ensuring compliance and simplifying financial management for S Corporations.
- For C Corporations: The complexity of C Corporations demands a software solution that offers detailed financial reporting, robust tax planning tools, and scalability. NetSuite ERP emerges as a powerful contender, providing an all-encompassing suite of tools designed to meet the complex requirements of C Corporations, from financial management to compliance reporting.

Selecting the right bookkeeping software for your business is not just about the features it offers today but how well it can grow and adapt with you. Your choice should be a catalyst for efficiency, clarity, and strategic decision-making, enabling you to focus on steering your business toward its goals. Whether you're a solo entrepreneur charting your course, a partnership navigating shared ambitions, or a corporation plotting a course through the complexities of the corporate world, the right bookkeeping software is an indispensable companion on your journey to success.

11.3 COMPLIANCE AND REPORTING

Navigating the landscape of tax obligations and reporting requirements demands a map updated with the latest regulatory landmarks for each business structure. This section is tailored to provide that map, guiding small business owners through the maze of compliance with finesse. It's about turning what often seems like a daunting task into a series of manageable steps, ensuring your business meets its legal obligations and thrives because of them.

Navigating Tax Obligations and Reporting Requirements

Each business structure wears unique tax obligations like a badge, defining its identity in the financial ecosystem. Understanding these obligations is crucial for those at the helm of their business ship.

Staying on top of compliance requires a calendar not just marked with holidays but pivotal financial deadlines:

- Annual Tax Filings: This is the moment each business structure accounts for its annual financial dance. From

Form 1040 Schedule C for sole proprietors to Form 1120 for C Corporations, ensuring these are filed accurately and on time is non-negotiable.

- Quarterly Estimated Tax Payments: For those structures where profits flow directly to the owners, such as sole proprietorships, partnerships, and S Corporations, quarterly payments are a rhythm that can't be missed. It's about keeping pace with your tax obligations throughout the year, avoiding the scramble when tax season arrives.
- Employment Tax Filings for S and C Corporations: Beyond income taxes, these entities must also navigate the waters of employment taxes, ensuring that forms like 941 and 940 are filed as required, reflecting payroll taxes withheld and paid.

In addition, compliance checklists often include state-specific filings, sales tax reporting for those engaged in direct sales, and local business permits and licenses. Each checklist item is a step towards ensuring your business operates within the legal framework, protecting it from potential penalties and legal complications.

Tips for Simplifying Compliance Through Effective Bookkeeping Practices

While the path of compliance may seem strewn with obstacles, integrating effective bookkeeping practices can clear the way:

- Automate Where Possible: Leveraging bookkeeping software that automates tax calculations, payroll processing, and even some aspects of compliance reporting can transform a tedious process into a streamlined operation. Automation reduces the risk of human error, ensuring accuracy in your financial reports.

- Maintain Impeccable Records: This cannot be overstated. Every transaction, no matter how small, needs to be documented. Digital bookkeeping solutions offer a centralized platform for storing receipts, invoices, and other transaction records, making it easier to pull information for tax filings or audits.
- Regular Reconciliation: Ensuring that your bookkeeping records match up with bank statements and other financial accounts monthly helps catch discrepancies early. This practice not only aids in accurate reporting but also provides insights into the financial health of your business.
- Consult with Professionals: Even with the best tools at your disposal, the complexity of tax laws and reporting requirements often necessitates professional guidance. Regular consultations with a CPA or a tax advisor can provide clarity, ensure compliance, and offer strategies for tax optimization.

Incorporating these practices into your financial management routine simplifies compliance and fortifies your business's financial integrity. It's about creating a framework within which your business operates smoothly, meeting its legal obligations while focusing on growth and profitability. Compliance and reporting, thus, become not just duties but integral parts of your business strategy, contributing to its long-term success.

11.4 PLANNING FOR GROWTH AND RESTRUCTURING

The business landscape is ever-evolving, and with growth comes the necessity to reassess and often recalibrate the foundational structure of your enterprise. As you stand at this crossroads, contemplating a shift in your business structure, it's crucial to recognize the ripple effects this decision will have on your book-keeping and tax obligations. This section aims to shed light on the intricacies of such a transition, offering a roadmap to navigate the complexities of growth and restructuring.

Impact on Bookkeeping and Taxes

A change in business structure is more than just a shift in operational dynamics; it's a transformation that extends into the financial veins of your organization, affecting bookkeeping practices and tax responsibilities.

- Bookkeeping Adjustments: Transitioning, for instance, from a sole proprietorship to an LLC introduces a new layer of financial recording. Where once a single-entry system might have sufficed, the complexity of transactions in an LLC might necessitate adopting a double-entry bookkeeping system, ensuring accuracy in financial records that now reflect the interests of multiple members.
- Tax Implications: The leap from an LLC to an S Corporation brings significant tax considerations. Electing S Corp status alters the tax landscape, shifting from pass-through taxation to a structure that mandates payroll tax compliance for shareholder-employees. This transition requires meticulous planning to optimize tax benefits while adhering to IRS compensation guidelines.

Steps for Transitioning Structures

Embarking on a restructuring journey demands a strategic approach, where every step is carefully planned to ensure a seamless transition.

- Legal and Financial Consultation: Begin by consulting with legal and financial experts familiar with the nuances of business structures. Their insights can help outline the benefits and drawbacks of the proposed change, ensuring the decision aligns with your long-term business goals.
- Notifying Relevant Authorities: Once a decision is made, informing the relevant state and federal authorities is important. This might involve filing new formation documents, updating licenses and permits, and ensuring compliance with state-specific requirements for the new structure.
- Updating Bookkeeping Systems: With the legal framework in place, the next step is to update your bookkeeping practices to reflect the new structure. This may include setting up new accounts, adjusting the chart of accounts, and implementing new software features or systems designed to handle the complexity of the new structure.
- Communicating with Stakeholders: Keeping stakeholders informed throughout the process is vital. Whether it's investors, employees, or clients, clear communication about the changes and how they impact the business relationship is crucial for maintaining trust and continuity.

Considerations for Future Growth and Scalability

As you lay the groundwork for your business's evolution, it's essential to anchor your bookkeeping practices in principles of growth and scalability.

- Future-Proofing Your Systems: Choose bookkeeping software and practices that fit today and can adapt to tomorrow's challenges. Look for solutions that offer scalability, automation, and integration capabilities, ensuring they can grow with your business.

- Scalable Tax Planning: Adopt a proactive approach to tax planning, considering immediate benefits and long-term tax implications. As your business scales, strategies that minimize tax liabilities while ensuring compliance can significantly impact financial health.
- Adapting to Operational Complexity: As your business structure evolves, so too will its operational complexity. Anticipate the need for more sophisticated bookkeeping and financial management practices, from detailed cost tracking to multi-tiered financial reporting, ensuring you have the systems and expertise to manage this complexity effectively.

In the dance of business growth and restructuring, each step forward requires thoughtful consideration of its impact on your bookkeeping and tax obligations. By planning meticulously for these transitions, you lay a solid foundation for your business to navigate the complexities of growth and thrive amidst them. With the right preparation, consultation, and strategic planning, you can steer your business toward a future marked by financial stability and success, ready to adapt to the evolving demands of the marketplace.

This journey through the financial landscape of small businesses, from the simplicity of sole proprietorships to the intricate dynamics of corporations, reveals a common thread: the need for clarity, precision, and strategic foresight in financial management. By choosing the right bookkeeping software, staying on top of compliance, and planning for growth and restructuring, you position your business for success in a competitive marketplace.

As you move forward, remember that the structure of your business is not just a legal designation; it's a blueprint for its financial and operational identity. Aligning your bookkeeping practices with this identity is not just about maintaining accurate records; it's about crafting a financial narrative that supports your vision, drives your strategy, and brings your business goals within reach.

With this foundation, you're well-equipped to navigate the challenges and opportunities ahead, turning your entrepreneurial aspirations into tangible outcomes.

Keeping the Game Alive

Now that you're armed with the tools to manage your finances, increase your profits, and streamline your taxes, it's your turn to light the way for others in search of guidance.

Leaving your honest feedback on Amazon not only helps other small business owners find the roadmap they need but also continues the cycle of shared success in the bookkeeping and financial management community.

Thank you for choosing to be a part of this journey. The legacy of financial literacy and empowerment grows stronger with each piece of knowledge passed forward.

>>> Click here to leave your review on Amazon (https://www.amazon.com/review/review-your-purchases/?asin=BOOKASIN).

Your contribution keeps the spirit of learning and growing alive, helping both me and the entire community to spread essential skills and insights. Thank you for making a difference.

CONCLUSION

As we draw the curtains on this enlightening journey from the foundational stones of bookkeeping to the strategic peaks of financial management, I reflect with pride on the path we've navigated together. You've evolved from grappling with the intricacies of financial jargon to mastering the vital arts of cash flow management, tax compliance, payroll intricacies, and strategies for financing growth. From feeling overwhelmed to becoming adept, this transformation marks a significant milestone in your journey as a small business owner.

The key takeaways we've explored emphasize the essence of demystifying complex financial concepts. The daily bookkeeping practices, the methodologies for managing cash flow with finesse, the confident navigation through the maze of tax obligations, and the pivotal role of strategic financial planning in creating business growth cannot be overstated.

I've worked to arm you with practical tools and strategies throughout our journey. The actionable tools, from financial document samples to tax planning checklists and software recommendations, have been carefully curated to bridge the gap between theoretical knowledge and real-world application. They are your compass and map in the intricate world of financial management.

Yet, the journey doesn't end here. The landscapes of regulatory frameworks and economic environments are ever-changing. I urge you to embrace continuous learning and adaptation as your allies. Remaining vigilant about regulatory changes, refining your bookkeeping practices with your business's growth, and persistently enriching your knowledge pool will fortify your financial management skills.

Now, I call upon you to take that bold first step toward implementing the strategies we've discussed. Whether it's inaugurating a new bookkeeping system, refining your tax planning, or instituting a cash flow enhancement plan, your action today is the cornerstone of your business's financial health tomorrow.

I understand the journey may seem daunting at times, but remember, mastering bookkeeping and financial management is within your grasp. Do not hesitate to seek professional guidance when necessary, and lean on the supportive online community of fellow entrepreneurs.

Envision a future where you are not just participating in the financial narrative of your business but directing it with confidence. A future where informed decisions lead to growth, stability, and success. This is not just a possibility but a reality within your reach.

I invite you to share your stories of triumphs and trials as you apply the principles outlined in this book. Your experiences enrich our collective journey and pave the way for future editions and resources tailored to your evolving needs.

Looking ahead, I am excited to explore specific facets of financial management more deeply through future books, workshops, or online courses. Stay connected to continue our shared journey of learning and growth.

With heartfelt gratitude, I thank you for entrusting me with the task of guiding you through the complexities of financial management. Your dedication to mastering these skills is commendable and speaks volumes of your commitment to your business's success. Together, let's continue to weave the fabric of financial literacy and empowerment, crafting a legacy of prosperity and resilience.

Here's to your continued success in navigating the financial waves, armed with knowledge, confidence, and the courage to chart your course.

REFERENCES

40 Accounting Terms Business Owners Should Know https://www.devry.edu/blog/ basic-accounting-terms-business-owners-should-know.html

Beginners' Guide to Financial Statement https://www.sec.gov/reportspubs/investor-publications/investorpubsbegfinstmtguide

Debits VS Credits: A Simple, Visual Guide https://www.bench.co/blog/bookkeeping/ debits-credits

A Small Business Guide to Payroll Deductions in 2024 https://www.fool.com/the-ascent/small-business/payroll/articles/payroll-deduction/

Cash vs Accrual Accounting: What's The Difference? https://www.forbes.com/advisor/ business/cash-vs-accrual-accounting/

Best Small Business Accounting Software of 2023 https://www.usnews.com/360-reviews/business/best-small-business-accounting-software

Chart of Accounts: A Small Business Guide https://www.fool.com/the-ascent/small-business/accounting/articles/chart-of-accounts/

The Essentials of Document Management in Accounting - Blog https://blog.rjyoung. com/document-management-systems/the-essentials-of-document-manage ment-in-accounting

Best Small Business Accounting Software of 2023 https://www.usnews.com/360-reviews/business/best-small-business-accounting-software

How to Use Double-Entry Accounting - The Motley Fool https://www.fool.com/the-ascent/small-business/accounting/articles/double-entry-accounting/#:

16 Essential Invoicing Tips For Small Businesses to Grow https://www.invensis.net/ blog/tips-for-effective-invoicing-for-businesses

7 Smart Ways To Manage Cash Flow In Your Small Business https://www.forbes.com/ sites/melissahouston/2023/04/25/7-smart-ways-to-manage-cash-flow-in-your-small-business/

The Definitive Guide to Small Business Cash Flow https://www.runviably.com/ resources/guide-to-small-business-cash-flow/

Cash Flow Forecast Planning Software for SMBs in 2023 https://www.abacum.io/blog/ best-cash-flow-forecasting-software-for-smbs

7 cash flow problems (and solutions) for small businesses https://quickbooks.intuit.com/ r/cash-flow/cash-flow-problems/

Cash Flow Analysis: The Basics - Investopedia https://www.investopedia.com/articles/ stocks/07/easycashflow.asp

Small-Business Tax Changes and Tips to Know in 2023 https://www.nerdwallet.com/article/small-business/small-business-taxes-2023

Recordkeeping | Internal Revenue Service https://www.irs.gov/businesses/small-busi nesses-self-employed/recordkeeping

17 Big Tax Deductions (Write Offs) for Businesses https://www.bench.co/blog/tax-tips/small-business-tax-deductions

IRS Audits | Internal Revenue Service https://www.irs.gov/businesses/small-busi nesses-self-employed/irs-audits

9 Best Payroll Services For Small Business (2024) https://www.forbes.com/advisor/business/software/best-payroll-services/

Payroll Taxes: A Guide for Small Business Owners https://blog.flock.com/payroll-taxes-a-guide-for-small-business-owners

Setting Up an Employee Benefits Program in 5 Steps https://fitsmallbusiness.com/setting-up-employee-benefits/

Outsourcing Payroll: Pros and Cons for Businesses https://www.indeed.com/hire/c/info/outsourcing-payroll

7 Effective Budgeting Tips for Small Business https://www.volopay.com/blog/budget ing-tips-for-small-businesses/

The Best Small Business Financing Options, Compared https://www.fundera.com/busi ness-loans/guides/small-business-financing

What Is Good Debt and Bad Debt for a Small Business? https://www.uschamber.com/co/run/finance/good-vs-bad-debt-for-small-business

Best Accounting Software for Small Business of 2024 https://www.investopedia.com/best-accounting-software-for-small-business-5069679

Best Accounting Software for Small Businesses of ... https://www.nerdwallet.com/best/small-business/accounting-software

How to Integrate Your Payroll and Accounting Software https://www.techrepublic.com/article/how-to-integrate-payroll-accounting-software/

Small Business Industry Financial Benchmark Data Library https://www.projection hub.com/post/small-business-industry-benchmark-data

Top Five Advanced Tax-Planning Strategies For Entrepreneurs https://www.forbes.com/sites/forbesbusinesscouncil/2021/02/25/top-five-advanced-tax-plan ning-strategies-for-entrepreneurs/

7 Smart Ways To Manage Cash Flow In Your Small Business https://www.forbes.com/sites/melissahouston/2023/04/25/7-smart-ways-to-manage-cash-flow-in-your-small-business/

10 Top Financial Challenges for Small Businesses and ... https://www.netsuite.com/portal/resource/articles/business-strategy/small-business-financial-challenges.shtml

How Financial Advisors Can Help Small Business https://www.investopedia.com/arti

cles/fa-profession/092516/financial-advisors-should-cater-small-business-needs.asp

Building A Business Emergency Fund: 5 Steps For Startups https://www.zeni.ai/blog/business-emergency-fund

Internal Revenue Service (IRS)
Website: https://www.irs.gov
Description: A primary source for individuals and businesses to find information regarding tax obligations and implications for various business structures. The IRS website offers a wide range of tax-related resources, forms, and guides to assist taxpayers in complying with federal tax laws.

U.S. Small Business Administration (SBA)
Website: https://www.sba.gov
Description: Provides comprehensive guides and resources on different business structures, including their operational and financial management implications. The SBA supports entrepreneurs and small business owners with tools for planning, launching, managing, and growing their business.

SCORE
Website: https://www.score.org
Description: Offers mentoring and workshops focusing on financial management and bookkeeping for various types of businesses. SCORE connects entrepreneurs with volunteer mentors to help solve business challenges and seize new opportunities.

National Federation of Independent Business (NFIB)
Website: https://www.nfib.com
Description: Offers a range of resources and articles on financial management best practices tailored to different business structures. NFIB is an advocacy organization representing small and independent businesses' interests.

QuickBooks Resource Center
Website: https://quickbooks.intuit.com/r/
Description: Contains articles, guides, and tips on setting up and managing bookkeeping for various business models. This resource center is aimed at helping business owners streamline their financial processes with QuickBooks software.

FreshBooks Blog
Website: https://www.freshbooks.com/blog
Description: Provides insights and tips on financial management specifically tailored to small businesses and freelancers. Topics cover various structures, aiming to improve financial literacy and management skills among entrepreneurs.

Made in the USA
Columbia, SC
18 May 2024